"*For the Love of Children* is perfect for people who want kids and people who have kids. It's ideal for a gift to give and to get! I'll buy them by the dozen."

—Jeannie Cheatham
author and award-winning jazz and blues pianist and vocalist

"Reading *For the Love of Children* is like walking into a room full of people from the past and present, from all walks of life, all talking about children and parenting. This collection of quotes and essays is thought-provoking, laugh-provoking and love-provoking. What a perfect book for new parents! . . . Old parents! . . . Heck, I don't even have kids and I'd buy it."

—Janell Cannon
author, *Stellaluna* and *Verde*

"Anyone who reads Eva Shaw's *For the Love of Children* will raise their own with more love, more patience, more joy and more awe at the responsibility and opportunity to make a difference, not only in their child's life, but for all the generations to come. What a wonderful book to own and to give!"

—Natasha Josefowitz, M.S.W., Ph.D.
adjunct professor, San Diego State University
and author of *Too Wise to Want to Be Young Again*

"This book is a unique and priceless reference about raising children that has something to think about and smile about on every page. It reassures parents and reaffirms to grandparents that raising children is timeless. It is easy to read, quotable and fun."

—Bryan Judge
president, Institute of Children's Literature

"This is a wonderful book for parents, teachers and other writers. I found the quotes and stories about children and families simply delightful. . . . I will use them in cards to my children, letters to friends, and Post-it Notes above my workspace as a gentle reminder that children, all children, are the greatest of gifts in life and should be counted as our most valuable treasures."

—Donna Guthrie
author, *The Witch Who Lives Down the Hall, Nobiah's Well* and *Frankie Murphy's Kiss List*

"Parenthood radically changes a person. Raising a child is exhausting, exasperating, expensive. It's also been the most gratifying experience of my life. I wrote a book to explain all that. This wonderful book celebrates it."

—Jacqueline Shannon
columnist, *Cosmopolitan* magazine and author,
The New Mother's Body Book and *Why It's Great to Be a Girl*

"Inspiring piece of literature. Gives you hope for the human race. Children are our future."

—Linda L. Schulte, Ed.D.

D0047894

"Imagine convening a congress of the world's greats . . . from poets to punsters . . . from philosophers to funny men and women . . . from 200 B.C. to the end of the 20th century . . . and then . . .

"Imagine the fun of asking those assembled sages for their wisest words and clever comments about living with and for children . . .

"Imagine the variety: humor, pathos, joy, irony, how-to's, and haikus . . . advice and anecdotes and amusing one-liners.

"Imagine no more! Eva Shaw's *For the Love of Children* has arrived to share the wisdom of the world in delicious bites."

—Joan Hansen
founder and chairperson, Orange County Festival of Women Authors and the Children's Author Festivals

"This book reinforces the values that set the path of our journey through life with children. I related to the quotes and stories as if they were passages from my life with my own children. I laughed and cried and said a prayer of thanks for the wonderful human beings my four children are. I believe every reader will reap the same reward; coming away loving their children even more. Warm, happy, fulfilled and thankful: these are the feelings I had when I finished *For the Love of Children*."

—Sheila Cluff
fitness expert, owner of The Oaks at Ojai and The Palms at Palm Springs, California, health and fitness spas

"*For the Love of Children* is a delightful collection of insights, instructions and humor rolled into one nice, neat package. As a mother, I found myself nodding to the quips and sayings. The entire book reflects the positive advantages of parenting and children."

—Sandy Whelchel
executive director, The National Writers Association

"*For the Love of Children* should be required reading for expectant moms and dads. If only it could be used as a refresher course for those of us who are lucky enough to be parents, grandparents, aunts and uncles. Eva sketches parenthood as it is: The most joyful and divine, baffling and infuriating time of adults' lives. Her book let me revisit the delights of my own children's toothless smiles, skinned knees, sticky fingers and cherished childhood moments that are etched forever in my heart."

—Ali Lassen
author, speaker and founder of Leads Club, the world's largest networking organization

"Eva Shaw's thoughtful and sensitive collection of reflections on children and the adults who care for them is laced with humor and delight for the children around us and the children in all of us. She has gently reminded me of why I have given thirty years of my life toward caring for children. She draws you 'home' to the richness of being a child through her carefully woven fabric of 'heart talk' that speaks to us 'for the love of children'."

—Cheryl Ernst
superintendent, Carlsbad Unified School District, past president of the Association of California School Administrators

For the L♥ve of Children

Eva Shaw

Health Communications, Inc.
Deerfield Beach, Florida

www.hci-online.com

We would like to thank the publishers and individuals who granted us permission to reprint the cited material.

"How to Perfect Maternal Feelings of Guilt." From SPECIAL DELIVERY by Shirley Jackson. ©1960 by Little, Brown and Company (Inc.). By permission Little, Brown and Company.

"A Letter to My Chosen Child." Reprinted by permission of Alice S. Ross. ©1995 Alice S. Ross.

"A Little Peach in the Orchard Grew." From *The New Guest Room Book.* ©1957 by Sheed & Ward. Reprinted by permission of Sheed & Ward, 115 E. Armour Blvd., Kansas City, MO 64111.

Library of Congress Cataloging-in-Publication Data

For the love of children / [edited by] Eva Shaw.
    p.   cm.
    Includes bibliographical references and indexes.
    ISBN 1-55874-550-5 (pbk.)
    1. Children—Literary collections. 2. Children—Quotations. I.
Shaw, Eva.
PN6071.C5F57   1998   97-40969
808.88'2—dc21   CIP

Publisher: Health Communications, Inc.
              3201 S.W. 15th Street
              Deerfield Beach, Florida 33442-8190

Cover design by Lawna P. Oldfield
Cover photo by CeCe Canton

Contents

Introduction

Like the conception of a baby, books are produced through a spark that is too magical to describe, but from which all of the universe has been created.

It is, once more like birth, that a book is born and released to humanity, and this book has become a dear, fulfilling part of my life. I feel much like the parent as this book goes out into the community of the world. I watched helplessly, naked in the public scrutiny, as my "baby" moved along the publishing process and eventually into your hands.

Never truly out of my heart or memory, I once more sense those feelings of loss and unending pride, closely compared to seeing my five-year-old climb on that enormous, ugly baby-snatching monster — the yellow school bus. I am again a trembling parent, knowing that before the day's end, my child will have experienced a few scrapes and maybe tragedy and uninhibited laughter. As he trots up the bus steps, I know in my heart that he is actually walking through the portal marked "Enter here to grow up." Then,

in another second, years slip away. Suddenly, I am that pet-
rified, fortyish mother now waving good-bye to a blithe,
unaware freshman, who has for the last year been counting
the minutes until college starts.

There is as much breath-holding in writing as there is in
parenthood, and one cannot ever really be prepared to bring
a new child or a new book to the examination or apprecia-
tion of humankind. There's never a perfect time, and words
often fail when they are needed most. A parent and a writer
share the same hopes, fears, prayers and dreams.

Like children, books take on a magical personality unique
unto themselves. With its collection of quotes, verse, opinions and essays, this book was nurtured from a spark to
encompass extraordinary characteristics well beyond those
initially conceived. It took on a nature of its own. Like
childhood, it is as powerful as it is lonely. It is funny. It is
joyful, and it is thoughtful and it is provocative. It is the sum
of all parts—heredity at its best—a combination plate of the
practical and a buffet of whimsy.

My publishers at Health Communications, my agent
Doris Michaels, and my friend and editor Jackie Landis
have been the catalysts for this project. It has been their
dream, too. Personally, it is my desire that the book will
continue to inspire and assist parents and grandparents and
people who love children well past the time when, perhaps,
if we're very fortunate, we'll have lots of grandkids to spoil.

My husband, Joe, and our son, Matt, remain my solid rock
of reality. They fortify life by teasing me back to the "here of
today," and by always having time to listen to the latest snip-
pet of philosophy or quirky bit of sense or nonsense I've

uncovered or embraced. To those who have encouraged, assisted and simply been there, I thank you.

To all who need one more reason to thank the universe for the incredible gift of childhood, for children and their unblemished (yet sometimes somewhat tarnished) love, I dedicate this book.

And most of all, I dedicate this book to Tiffany, a granddaughter who is a gift beyond price.

A baby is God's opinion that the world should go on.

—Carl Sandburg

In every child who is born, under no matter what circumstances, and of no matter what parents, the potentiality of the human race is born again; and in him, too, once more, and of each of us, our terrific responsibility towards human life; towards the utmost idea of goodness, of the horror of error; and, of God.

—James Agee

There are better things than curfews to bring kids home and off the streets at night: a mother singing in the kitchen and a dad whistling around the house.

—Burton Hills

Being a parent used to be one of the most simple, natural, inevitable developments in the world. But, nowadays, one has no business to be married unless, waking and sleeping, one is conscious of the responsibility.

—Dr. Abraham Flexner

In the effort to give good and comforting answer to the questioners whom we love, we very often arrive at good and comforting answers for ourselves.

—Ruth Goode

When you are a mother, you are never really alone in your thoughts. You are connected to your child and to all those who touch your lives. A mother always has to think twice, once for herself and once for her child.

—*Sophia Loren*

I looked on child-rearing not only as a work of love and duty but as a profession that was fully as interesting and challenging as any honorable profession in the world, and one that demanded the best that I could bring to it.

—*Rose Kennedy*

If we want better people to make a better world, then we will have to begin where people are made . . . in the family.

—*Anonymous*

If there were no other reasons (though we know there are as many as stars), this alone would be the value of children: the way they remind you of the comfort of simplicity. Their compelling common sense. Their accessibility and their honesty. Their lack of pretense.

—*Elizabeth Berg*

Insanity is hereditary; you can get it from your children.

—*Sam Levenson*

They who educate children well, are more to be honored than they who produce them; for these only gave them life, those the art of living well.

—Aristotle

It goes without saying that you should never have more children than you have car windows.

—Erma Bombeck

When you look at your life, the greatest happiness is family happiness.

—Dr. Joyce Brothers

To nourish children and raise them against odds is in any time, any place, more valuable than to fix bolts in cars or design nuclear weapons.

—Marilyn French

After you have children, the economic law reverses to Demand and Supply.

—Marcelene Cox

The Children's Hour

by Henry Wadsworth Longfellow

Between the dark and the daylight,
When the night is beginning to lower,
Comes a pause in the day's occupations,
That is known as the Children's Hour.

I hear in the chamber above me,
The patter of little feet,
The sounds of a door that is opened,
And voices soft and sweet.

From my study I see in the lamplight,
Descending the broad hall stair,
Grave Alice, and laughing Allegra,
And Edith with golden hair.

A whisper, and then a silence:
Yet, I know by their merry eyes
They are plotting and planning together
To take me by surprise.

A sudden rush from the stairway,
A sudden raid from the hall!
By three doors left unguarded
They enter my castle wall!

They climb up into my turret,
O'er the arms and back of my chair;
If I try to escape, they surround me;
They seem to be everywhere.

They almost devour me with kisses,
Their arms about me entwine,
Till I think of the Bishop of Bingen
In his Mouse-Tower on the Rhine!

Do you think, O blue-eyed banditti,
Because you have scaled the wall,
Such an old mustache as I am
Is not a match for you all!

I have you fast in my fortress,
And will not let you depart,
but put you down in the dungeon
In the round-tower of my heart.

And there will I keep you forever,
Yes, forever and a day,
Till the walls shall crumble in ruin,
And moulder in dust away!

Nothing has a stronger influence psychologically on their environment, and especially on their children, than the unlived life of the parents.

—C. G. Jung

Don't limit a child to your own learning, for he was born in another time.

—Rabbinic Proverb

Truth, which is important to a scholar, has got to be concrete. And there is nothing more concrete than dealing with babies, burps, and bottles, frogs and mud.

—Jeanne J. Kirkpatrick

Joy of parenthood: What grown-ups feel when the kids are in bed.

—Anonymous

Heaven lies about us in our infancy!

—William Wordsworth

A child's world is fresh and new and beautiful, full of wonder and excitement. It is our misfortune that for most of us that clear-eyed vision, that true instinct for what is beautiful and awe-inspiring, is dimmed and even lost before we reach adulthood.

If I had influence with the good fairy who is supposed to preside over the christening of all children, I should ask that her gift to each child in the world be a sense of wonder so indestructible that it would last throughout life, as an unfailing antidote against boredom and disenchantments of later years, the sterile preoccupation with things that are artificial, the alienation from the sources of our strength.

—*Rachel Carson*

Family jokes, though rightly cursed by strangers, are the bond that keeps most families alive.

—*Stella Benson*

Ask your child what he wants for dinner only if he's buying.

—*Fran Lebowitz*

The Starting Line

by Bonnie Prudden

The three best years for building an excellent body, patterns and attitudes come between birth and three. In those years all that a person will be is formed.

Many people working with children take exception to this, but studies show that in this respect children can be likened to furniture. When you decide to build a chair, you must start from the first moment building a chair. Its purpose is decided. After its form is laid down and glued together, it is a chair, not a table, not a dresser, not a lamp . . . a chair. That parallels the first three years for children.

You can paint the chair, upholster it, add a cushion, casters, even wheels. It is still a chair. You can similarly educate children, give them goals, a profession, all kinds of skills, but the initial person beneath is still the one put together in those first years. The optimist, the pessimist, the unsure, the timid, the outgoing and the skeptic all formed early.

Once the children were in the house the air became more vivid and more heated; every object in the house grew more alive.

—Mary Gordon

Seeing you sleeping peacefully on your back, among your stuffed ducks, bears and basset hounds, would remind me that no matter how good the next day might be, certain moments were gone forever because we could not go backwards in time.

—Joan Baez

Children are unpredictable. You never know what inconsistency they're going to catch you at next.

—Franklin P. Jones

If a growing object is both fresh and spoiled at the same time, chances are it is a child.

—Morris Goldfischer

The World Through Three Senses
by Helen Keller

I am not a teacher or an educator, but I have always believed that infants should be taught as soon as possible, before they speak, to notice objects pretty or delightful or unusual. I have noted the wholesome effect upon a baby of fixing his eyes upon a pleasing color or a delicately carved shell, listening to music that soothes or enchants him, touching a face he loves or smelling a flower to which he smiles.

If the mother puts as much gentle art into this delicate fostering of all his physical powers as she does into the task of preserving his health, her reward will be past calculating. The child's five senses are the faithful fairies who, if cherished and heeded, will surrender to him their priceless tokens of royalty—the splendor at the rainbow's end, the seven-league books of imagination, lovely dreams fulfilled. He will always be charged or comforted by sky, earth and sea. Not only will he reach a well-ordered stewardship of his senses, he will also have the best chance of spiritual maturity.

For there is, I am convinced, a correspondence between the powers of the body and those of the spirit, and when the five senses—or whatever of them there are—serve as entrances into an inner world, the individual attains his or her fullest capacity of pleasure as well as self-mastery. Every person, every group thus excellently equipped for living is the greatest possible contribution to humanity. That is why I like to celebrate the accomplishments of the handicapped whom necessity drives to us all the faculties that remain. They show that normal beings can and should do with a complete set of faculties.

Once parents and teachers realize the tremendous potencies of good folded up in sense-life and set about developing them in children, they will confer upon the coming generation a blessing that will carry through untold ages its multiplying harvests of alertness, strength and beauty of life.

What the mother sings to the cradle goes all the way down to the coffin.

—Henry Ward Beecher

The time to start correcting children is before they begin to correct you.

—Anonymous

If the family were a sport, it would be baseball: a long, slow, nonviolent game that is never over until the last out.

—Letty Cottin Pogrebin

Every love relationship hits some hard times, and the loving relationship between parents and their children is no exception.

—Ava L. Siegler, Ph.D.

With any child entering adolescence, one hunts for signs of health, is desperate for the smallest indication that the child's problems will never have been important enough for a television movie.

—Delia Ephron

People who say they sleep like a baby usually don't have one.

—Leo J. Burke

Now the first thing about having a baby—and I can't be the first person to have noticed this—is that thereafter you have it.

—Jean Kerr

In the sheltered simplicity of the first days after a baby is born, one sees again the magical closed circle. The miraculous sense of two people existing only for each other.

—Anne Morrow Lindbergh

For a growing child, eternity is the interval between getting home and seeing supper on the table.

—Anonymous

A child prodigy is one with highly imaginative parents.

— Will Rogers

Brave New Electronic World
by Art Linkletter

When I was a boy, my hero was Buck Rogers, the invincible spaceman of the comic pages. But now spaceships have soared out of the fantasy of the comings and into the headlines of reality . . . even old Buck's ray gun is being perfected in laboratories, as scientists continue to master the energies of light.

The world of kids has changed, too, since my generation learned to read and write. The little red schoolhouse has all but disappeared, and with it the old pot-bellied stove that stood in the corner, and the rows of desks with initials and valentine hearts carved all over them. Schools built today have air conditioning, scientific lighting, motion pictures and TV.

It all seems so different—but the kids themselves haven't changed at all. They may talk about their model jet planes and atomic submarines at recess, but they're still struggling the same way their mothers and fathers did to see the grown-up world right side up.

Some are kissing mothers and some are scolding mothers, but it is love just the same, and most mothers kiss and scold together.

—*Pearl S. Buck*

For years we have given scientific attention to the care and rearing of plants and animals, but we have allowed babies to be raised chiefly by tradition.

—*Edith Belle Lowry*

In the Indian way, everything is for the children. They learn respect because we show respect for them; we let them be free but at the same time, there is always someone there to teach them how to act, the right way to treat people.

—*Matthew King*

One of the luckiest things that can happen to you in life is, I think, to have a happy childhood.

—*Agatha Christie*

The Birthday Child

by A. E. Bray

Monday's child is fair of face,
Tuesday's child is full of grace,
Wednesday's child is full of woe,
Thursday's child has far to go,
Friday's child is loving and giving,
Saturday's child works hard for its living.
And the child that's born on the Sabbath day
Is fair and wise and good and gay.

Most mothers are instinctive philosophers.

—Harriet Beecher Stowe

Because I am a mother, I am capable of being shocked: as I never was when I was not one.

—Margaret Atwood

If men had to have babies they would only ever have one each.

—Diana, Princess of Wales

Is nothing in life ever straight and clear, the way children see it?

—Rosie Thomas

Even when freshly washed and relieved of all obvious confections, children tend to be sticky.

—Fran Lebowitz

Children are likely to live up to what you believe of them.

—*Lady Bird Johnson*

The difference of the soul/spirit dimensions of being with children is the difference from pretty to beautiful, from cute to enchanting, from interesting to awesome, from respect to reverence.

—*Carol Mankiti*

Childhood is the kingdom where nobody dies.

—*Edna St. Vincent Millay*

Our Lady Teaches Her Son
by Monsignor Ronald Knox

God became Man, to remake his world; he became a little child, and I suppose he used to play games; I don't think the Sacred Humanity would have been quite human if our Lord had never played games. And the best playmate he had, if so, was his Blessed Mother, such a short distance away from girlhood herself, who was so good at sympathizing, at seeing other people's points of view. At any rate, she was the Wisdom which accompanied him through all those steps of early childhood. Our Lord had, if he cared to use it, all the knowledge which is enjoyed by the blessed Saints in heaven. But, in order to be perfectly Man, he preferred to acquire knowledge by experience and by hearsay, just as you and I do. He went to school in the carpenter's shop; but his education had begun long before that. He had been learning all the time, "increasing in wisdom," the gospel tells us. And the person who taught him that wisdom was his mother—who else should it be? . . .

You have to think of a mother and her little son, who is just learning to talk in words of one syllable. They are looking out, from some point a bit west of Nazareth, at the great mass of Mount Carmel dominating the plain. And the boy asks, "Ma zeh?" [What's that?]. And his mother answers, "That's ha-har [the mountain]; say 'Har,' Jesus." Or they are a bit east of Nazareth, and suddenly through a gap in the hills they are looking down, across precipitous miles, at the Lake of Galilee where it forms a blue floor at the bottom of the plain. And this time she says, "Ha-yam [the sea]; say 'Yam,' Jesus." Or she takes him with her in the cool of the evening when she carries a jug to draw water at the spring called the Fountain of the Virgin, after her. And this time she says, "Ha-'em [the spring]; say 'Em,' Jesus." So the mind-pictures of the Incarnate were formed; and when he preached, years later, about a city set on a hill, or fishermen casting their nets into the sea, or a spring of water welling up to eternal life, he was utilizing the wisdom he had learned from that wise playmate of his, long ago.

A little boy, kneeling at bedside, asked his mother standing near, "Momma, do you think it would be okay if I put in a short commercial break for a new bike?"

—Eva Shaw

Mankind owes to the child the best it has to give.

—United Nations Declaration

Call it a clan, call it a network, call it a tribe, call it a family. Whatever you call it, whoever you are, you need one.

—Jane Howard

Parenthood is tough. If you just want a wonderful little creature to love, you can get a puppy.

—Barbara Walters

No animal is so inexhaustible as an excited infant.

—Amy Leslie

By the time the youngest children have learned to keep the house tidy, the oldest grandchildren are on hand to tear it to pieces.

—Christopher Morley

A mother is neither cocky, nor proud, because she knows the school principal may call at any minute to report that her child had just driven a motorcycle through the gymnasium.

—Mary Kay Blakely

The race of children possess magically sagacious powers!

—Gail Godwin

Family life! The United Nations is child's play compared with the tugs and splits and need to understand and forgive in any family.

—May Sarton

READER/CUSTOMER CARE SURVEY

If you are enjoying this book, please help us serve you better and meet your changing needs by taking a few minutes to complete this survey. Please fold it & drop it in the mail.

Name: _____

Address: _____

_____

Tel. # _____

As a special **"Thank You"** we'll send you exciting news about interesting books and a valuable Gift Cerificate. *It's Our Pleasure to Serve You!*

(1) Gender: 1) ____ Female 2) ____ Male

(2) Age:
1)____ 18-25 4)____ 46-55
2)____ 26-35 5)____ 56-65
3)____ 36-45 6)____ 65+

(3) Marital status:
1)____ Married 3)____ Single 5)____ Widowed
2)____ Divorced 4)____ Partner

(4) Is this book:
1)____ Purchased for self?
2)____ Purchased for others?
3)____ Received as gift?

(5) How did you find out about this book?
1)____ Catalog 2)____ Store Display
Newspaper
3)____ Best Seller List
4)____ Article/Book Review
5)____ Advertisement
Magazine
6)____ Feature Article
7)____ Book Review
8)____ Advertisement
9)____ Word of Mouth
A)____ T.V./Talk Show (Specify) _____
B)____ Radio/Talk Show (Specify) _____
C)____ Professional Referral _____
D)____ Other (Specify) _____

(6) What subject areas do you enjoy reading most? (Rank in order of enjoyment)
1)____ Women's Issues/   5)____ New Age/
       Relationships   Altern. Healing
2)____ Business Self Help 6)____ Aging
3)____ Soul/Spirituality/ 7)____ Parenting
       Inspiration   8)____ Diet/Nutrition/
4)____ Recovery   Exercise/Health

(14) What do you look for when choosing a personal growth book?
(Rank in order of importance)
1)____ Subject   3)____ Author
2)____ Title   4)____ Price
       Cover Design 5)____ In Store Location

(19) When do you buy books?
(Rank in order of importance)
1)____ Christmas
2)____ Valentine's Day
3)____ Birthday
4)____ Mother's Day
5)____ Other (Specify _____

(23) Where do you buy your books?
(Rank in order of frequency of purchases)
1)____ Bookstore   6)____ Gift Store
2)____ Price Club   7)____ Book Club
3)____ Department Store 8)____ Mail Order
4)____ Supermarket/   9)____ T.V. Shopping
       Drug Store   A)____ Airport
5)____ Health Food Store

Which Health Communications book are you currently reading? _____

Additional comments you would like to make to help us serve you better.

_____

_____

Thank You !!

The Little Hurts

by Edgar A. Guest

Every night she runs to me
With a bandaged arm or a bandaged knee,
A stone-bruised heel or a swollen brow,
And in sorrowful tones she tells me how
    She fell and "hurted herse'f to-day"
While she was having the "bestest play."

And I take up in my arms and kiss
The new little wounds and whisper this:
"Oh, you must be careful, my little one,
You mustn't get hurt while your daddy's gone,
    For every cut with its ache and smart
Leaves another bruise on your daddy's heart."

Every night I must stoop to see
The fresh little cuts on her arm or knee;
The little hurts that have marred her play,
And brought the tears on a happy day;
    For the path of childhood is oft beset
With care and trouble and things that fret.

Oh, little girl, when you older grow,
Far greater hurts than these you'll know;
    Greater bruises will bring you tears,

Around the bend of the lane of years,
But come to your daddy with them at night
And he'll do his best to make all things right.

Perhaps we have been misguided into taking too much responsibility from our children, leaving them too little room for discovery.

—*Helen Hayes*

Child psychology: what children manage parents with.

—*Eva Shaw*

Adults are always telling young people, "These are the best years of your life." Are they? I don't know. Sometimes when adults say this to children I look into their faces. They look like someone on the top seat of the Ferris wheel who has had too much cotton candy and barbecue. They'd like to get off and be sick but everyone keeps telling them what a good time they're having.

—*Erma Bombeck*

The suspicious parent makes an artful child.

—*Thomas C. Haliburton*

You know children are growing up when they start asking questions that don't have answers.

—John J. Plomp

Boys and girls need chances to be around their father, to be enjoyed by him and if possible to do things with him. Better to play fifteen minutes enjoyably and then say, "Now I'm going to read the paper" than to spend all day at the zoo crossly.

—Dr. Benjamin Spock

The real menace in dealing with a five-year-old is that in no time at all you begin to sound like a five-year-old.

—Jean Kerr

Remember when your mother used to say, "Go to your room!"? This was a terrible penalty. Now when a mother says the same thing, a kid goes to his room. There he's got an air conditioner, a TV set, an intercom, a shortwave radio—he's better off than he was in the first place.

—Sam Levenson

If a child lives with approval, he learns to live with himself.

—*Dorothy Law Nolte*

If you don't want your children to hear what you're saying, pretend you're talking to them.

—*Anonymous*

All parents think their children are gifted, and all children think their parents are mildly to severely mentally challenged.

—*Eva Shaw*

I got more children than I can rightly take care of, but I ain't got more than I can love.

—*Ossie Guffy*

Most children think the nicest way to serve broccoli is to some other kid.

—*Anonymous*

Children need special love and feedback. Treat your children as if they are God's sweetest expression in your life and have come into your life to bless you.

Sometimes we treat them as if they are burdens, and because we cannot get rid of them we have to put up with them. Celebrate that they came into your life to open your heart. If you can treat them with tenderness and love them with openness and trust, you will have a Divine experience.

—Swami Shantanand Saraswati

If you must hold yourself up to your child as an object lesson (which is not necessary), hold yourself up as a warning and not as an example.

—George Bernard Shaw

A child is a being who gets almost as much fun out of a five-hundred-dollar set of swings as it does out of playing in a cardboard box or finding an earthworm.

—Anonymous

A Lonesome Boy

from The New York Times *(1900)*

The boy sat huddled so close to the woman in gray that everybody felt sure he belonged to her; so when he unconsciously dug his muddy shoes into the broadcloth skirt of his left-hand neighbor, she leaned over and said: "Pardon me, madam, will you kindly make your little boy square himself around? He is soiling my skirt with his muddy shoes."

The woman in gray blushed a little and nudged the boy away. "My boy?" she said. "My goodness, he isn't mine."

The boy squirmed uneasily. He was such a little fellow that he could not touch his feet to the floor, so he stuck them out straight in front of him, like pegs to hang things on, and looked at them deprecatingly.

"I am sorry I got your dress dirty," he said to the woman on his left. "I hope it will brush off."

"Oh, it doesn't matter," she said. Then as his eyes were still fastened on hers she added, "Are you going uptown alone?"

"Yes, ma'am," he replied. "I always go alone. There isn't anybody to go with me. Father is dead and Mother is dead. I live with Aunt Clara, in Harlem, but she says Aunt Anna ought to help do something for me, so once or twice a week, when she gets tired and wants to go to some place to get rested up, she sends me over to stay with Aunt Anna. I'm going there now. Sometimes I don't find Aunt Anna at home, but I hope she will be at home today, because it looks as if it is going to rain and I don't like to hang around in the street in the rain."

The woman felt something uncomfortable in her throat and she said, "You are a very little boy to be knocked about this way," rather unsteadily.

"Oh, I don't mind," he said. "I never get lost. But I get lonesome sometimes on the long trips, and when I see anybody that I think I would like to belong to, I scooge up close to her so I can make believe that I really do belong to her. This morning I was playing that I belong to that lady on the other side of me, and I forgot about my feet. That is why I got your dress dirty."

The woman put her arms around the tiny chap and "scooged" him up so close . . . and every other woman, who had heard his artless confidence, looked as if she would not only let him wipe his shoes on her best gown, but would rather he did it than not.

Children need love, especially when they do not deserve it.

—*Harold S. Hulbert*

Children can be conceptualized as mirrors. If love is given to them, they return it. If none is given, they have none to return. Unconditional love is reflected unconditionally, and conditional love is returned conditionally.

—*Ross Campbell, M.D.*

There's a wealthy Los Angeles entrepreneur who was worried about his adored eight-year-old daughter. Her interest in life seemed confined to just one subject: clothes. School studies lost when there was an opportunity to shop, talk about the latest styles or look at fashion magazines.

One afternoon she came home from school and casually reported that her class had been told the facts of life by an up-to-the-minute expert on sex.

"At last," breathed the parent to himself, "my child will acquire a new concept on life." Ready as any expectant parent, he asked, "So Honey, aren't there any questions that you want to ask me about all the things you learned today. . . ? You know you can ask me anything and even if I don't know, we can find out together."

The girl thought for just a moment and then replied, "Just one, Dad."

Dad held his breath and leaned forward. "Anything, Honey . . . now don't be embarrassed."

"Well, actually, Dad . . . "

The father held his breath, as she continued: "What does a girl wear for that sort of thing?"

—*Eva Shaw*

Problems on Stereotyped Sex Roles

by Nancy C. A. Roeske, M.D.

At the birth of a new baby, most parents would answer the question of what they would like their child to be when he or she grows up by saying, "I want my child to be happy, to be whatever he or she wants to be."

We want our children to be creative and self-expressive, and society needs fully creative individuals. One way to help ensure that these goals are reached is to encourage our children to follow their own interests, regardless of whether or not these interests are deemed traditionally "appropriate" to his or her own sex.

Give me the children until they are seven and anyone may have them afterwards.

—*Saint Francis Xavier (1506-1552)*

If you've never seen a real, fully developed look of disgust, just tell your son how you conducted yourself when you were a boy.

—*Kin Hubbard*

Everyone is the Child of the past.

—*Edna G. Rostow*

In this day of rampant consumerism, you might be intimidated into believing that you will be seen as a less-than-perfect grandparent if you cannot afford to give your grandchild a special present for every occasion and during every visit. With all the important roles that grandmas and grandpas play in teaching their grandchildren about respect and love and finding their way in the world, nothing could be further from the truth.

If you love your grandchild and give . . . from your heart, he will return that love and respect regardless of the size of your pocketbook.

—*Lanie Carter*

A babe at the breast is as much pleasure as the bearing is pain.

—*Marion Zimmer Bradley*

Childhood had no forebodings; but then, it is soothed by no memories of outlived sorrow.

—*George Eliot*

To children, childhood holds no particular advantage.

—*Kathleen Norris*

A Good Friend

from The National Magazine Contest (1906)

To have a child who is a good friend is of the highest delights of life; to be a good friend to a child is one of the noblest and most difficult undertakings.

Friendship depends not upon fancy, imagination or sentiment, but upon character. There is no one so poor that he is not rich if he had a friend; there is no one so rich that he is not poor without a friend. But the friendship of one's child is more than can be encompassed in words or covered in a relationship. Real friendship is abiding. Like charity, it suffereth long and is kind. Like love, it vaunteth not itself, but pursues the even tenor of its way, unaffrighted by ill-report, loyal in adversity, the solvent of infelicity, the shining jewel of happy days.

Being friends with one's child has not the iridescent joy of love, though it is closer than is often known to the highest, truest love. Its heights are ever serene, its valleys know few clouds.

To aspire to friendship with one's child, one must cultivate a capacity for faithful affection, a beautiful disinterestedness, a clear discernment. Friendship is a gift, but it is also an acquirement. It is like the rope with which climbers in the high mountains bind themselves for safety, and only a coward cuts the rope when a comrade is in danger.

From Cicero to Emerson, and long before Cicero, and forever after Emerson, the praises of friendship have been set forth. Even fragments of friendship with one's child are precious and to be treasured. But to have a whole, real friend in one's child is the greatest of earth's gifts save one. To be a whole, real friend with one's child is a worthy high endeavor, for faith, truth, courage and loyalty bring one close to the kingdom of heaven.

Seven-year-old overheard talking to a pal as they are leaving the movies: "I like television better . . . it's not so far to the bathroom."

—Eva Shaw

Children are a great comfort in your old age—and they help you reach it faster, too.

—Lionel Kauffman

No child was probably ever loved too much. Many are indulged too much; some are spoiled in the name of love; but no child ever could have too much real genuine love, that deep and abiding affection that makes him feel wanted and secure and content. A child needs a great deal of this kind of love. She needs to know that she has it.

—Grace Langdon, Ph.D.

You have to love your children unselfishly: That's hard. But it's the only way.

—Barbara Bush

Notoriously insensitive to subtle shifts in mood, children will persist in discussing the color of a recently sighted cement-mixer long after one's own interest in the topic has waned.

—*Fran Lebowitz*

Somewhere around the age of twelve or thirteen, the little lad who has spent a dozen years driving his mother wild will suddenly become loving and helpful, kind and courteous. There is no reasonable explanation for this phenomenon; it may just be nature's way of balancing the sexual scales, for it is at this very age that Mommy's Sweetheart, the darling daughter who had never given a moment's concern, suddenly becomes stubborn, rebellious, self-righteous and bossy.

—*Teresa Bloomingdale*

The terrible twos: When a child is at the "no-it-all" stage.

—*Eva Shaw*

I know of no pleasure that quite matches that of seeing your youngster proudly flaunting something you have made.

—*Ruth Goode*

If you want a baby, have a new one. Don't baby the old one.

—*Jessamyn West*

Adolescence: the period of time when children feel their parents need to be told the facts of life.

—*Anonymous*

The time not to become a father is eighteen years before a world war.

—*E. B. White*

God knows that a mother needs fortitude and courage and tolerance and flexibility and patience and firmness and nearly every other brave aspect of the human soul. But because I happen to be a parent of almost fiercely maternal nature, I praise *casualness*. It seems to me the rarest of virtues. It is useful enough when children are small. It is important to the point of necessity when they are adolescents.

—*Phyllis McGinley*

Adorable children are considered to be the general property of the human race. (Rude children belong to their mothers.)

—Judith Martin (Miss Manners)

Nothing makes a child worse-behaved than knowing he belongs to a neighbor.

—Eva Shaw

A woman who can cope with the terrible twos can cope with anything.

—Judith Clabes

A lot of us who came of age in the 1960s are very wary of authority. But you can't be your child's friend; you have to turn into a parent.

—Wendy Schuman

Respect the child. Be not too much his parent. Trespass not on his solitude.

—Ralph Waldo Emerson

How can I teach, how can I save,
This child whose features are my own,
Whose feet run down the ways where I have walked?

—*Michael Roberts*

Any mother could perform the duties of several air-traffic controllers with ease.

—*Lisa Alther*

If children grew up according to early indicators, we should have nothing but geniuses.

—*Goethe*

A teen's grandmother said she'd like to buy the adolescent some CDs and wondered how to choose them. The reply came quickly. "Easy, Gram . . . just listen to them and if you can't stand the sound, I'll probably like 'em."

—*Eva Shaw*

There is nothing more thrilling in this world, I think, than having a child that is yours, and yet is mysteriously a stranger.

—Agatha Christie

A mother is not a person to lean on but a person to make leaning unnecessary.

—Dorothy Canfield Fisher

There's a time when you have to explain to your children why they were born, and it's a marvelous thing if you know the reason by then.

—Hazel Scott

The more you listen to your child's ideas and values—even those with which you don't agree—the more likely it is that your child will listen respectfully to the ideas and values of others, including your own.

—Lee Salk, M.D.

We've had bad luck with our kids—they're all grown up.

—Christopher Morley

What Makes a Home?
by John Lubbock

What makes a home? Love and sympathy and confidence. The memories of childhood, the kindness of parents, they bring hopes of youth, the sisters' pride, the brothers' sympathy and help, the mutual confidence, the common hopes and interests and sorrows; these create and sanctify the home.

Family faces are magic mirrors. Looking at people who belong to us, we see the past, present and future.

—*Gail Lumet Buckley*

It seems to me that since I've had children, I've grown richer and deeper. They may have slowed down my writing for a while, but when I did write, I had more of a self to speak from.

—*Anne Tyler*

Advice from parent to child: Think twice before you speak—especially if you intend to say what you think.

—*Eva Shaw*

We are taught you must blame your father, your sisters, your brothers, the school and the teachers—you can blame anyone, but never blame yourself. It's never your fault.

But it's always your fault because if you wanted to change, you're the one who has got to change. It's as simple as that, isn't it.

—*Katharine Hepburn*

Child psychology would be okay if you could just get the children to understand it.

—*Eva Shaw*

In bringing up children, spend on them half as much money and twice as much time.

—*Harold S. Hulbert*

Feel the dignity of a child. Do not feel superior to him, for you are not.

—*Robert Henri*

Strange

by Mildred Bowers Armstrong

Strange—to grow up and not be different,
Not beautiful or even very wise . . .
No winging-out the way of butterflies,
No sudden blindfold-lifting from the eyes.

Strange—to grow up and still be wondering
Reverent at petals and snow,
Still holding breath,
Still often tiptoe,
Questioning dew and stars,
Wanting to know!

Children's talent to endure stems from their ignorance of alternatives.

—*Maya Angelou*

So long as little children are allowed to suffer, there is no true love in the world.

—*Isadora Duncan*

There was a child went forth every day
And the first object he look'd upon,
That object he became.

— *Walt Whitman*

If you want to see what children can do, you must stop giving them things.

—*Norman Douglas*

How to Perfect Maternal Feelings of Guilt

by Shirley Jackson

Sooner or later you are going to be left alone with this baby. All alone, just you and Baby and an all-pervading panic.

You are reasonably sure by now that you are not going to sit down on him, or put the diaper over his head, but by golly, that is just about all you *are* sure of. Here is the same old place you have been living right along. There is the couch, and the table with the ashtray on it that your husband won playing golf in the Salesman's Tournament, and the curtains you made yourself, and the rug you still haven't paid for, and there is the kitchen with the dishes you have washed over and over again (standing by the sink, dreaming idly of what it would be like when Baby came, wondering if it would be a boy or a girl, standing there with the dishcloth in your hand and the soapsuds melting away) and the pots and pans and the little white enamel pan you bought for heating Baby's bottle. There is the bed you half-slept in all these months, longing to turn over and sleep on your stomach, promising yourself that once it was over and you could get a good night's sleep without the aching back, the aching ankles, the weary shoulders . . . oh, once it was over you would really *sleep* again. There are the clothes you have waited all this time to wear once more (Do they fit? No.) and the high-heeled shoes you haven't dared to put on yet.

There is the crib you set up so lovingly for Baby, you and his father, telling one another delightedly that Baby would lie *here,* and his little clothes would be put in *there,* and we can hear him if he makes the slightest noise at night. (Hear him? Get three blocks away and see if you can hear him make the slightest noise at night.) And *here* is where he'll have his bath, and *here* . . . well, here is Baby.

It's over. You can tie your shoes again. You can bend over to pick up a pin from the floor if you want to. You can sleep on your stomach again, except you've forgotten how to breathe sleeping on your stomach. The same dishes and pots and pans are there waiting to be washed, and waiting and waiting and waiting, while you try to find your way through the maze of the kitchen to get the little white enamel pot to heat up Baby's bottle. Baby is lying there, incredibly real and solid and pink, a real honest-to-goodness baby with all his arms and legs and toes and altogether beautiful and wonderful, possessing such breathtaking instinctive knowledge as how to close those small eyes and how to yawn (how does a baby yawn? Is it real?) and carrying somewhere within him the potential ability to grow a tooth, smile at his daddy, or reach out those small hands to his mother. And what is he doing, this baby, rich in infinite knowledge, full of beauty and wonder and delight, perfect and small and most incredibly of all—alive and individual? You know what he is doing.

The little eyes are closed all right, screwed tight shut. The perfect little hands are clenched, the pink little face is red with fury and the little mouth that will so soon grow teeth is wide open. The legs are kicking wildly, muscles that will someday be carrying him down a football field are rigid and tight, and he is making a racket altogether out of proportion to his size and strength. The nurses at the hospital knew what to do when he yelled like that. In the hospital they could always do something. He never yelled like this before. There must be something they forgot to tell you, some vital fact they all assumed you would know, some perfectly natural thing to do when Baby cries; perhaps there is something that normal maternal instinct would tell you right off ought to be done and because you are—oh, face it—not a normal mother, you don't know what this is—no one else's baby cries like this. There is something wrong with you; your baby is crying and you don't know what to do. Here everyone else knows what to do when a baby cries and there is something lacking in your makeup and you had no right to have children at all and the doctor should have told you instead of letting you go ahead and what will your mother say when she finds out you are some kind of a monster instead of a normal mother and maybe if you called the hospital and asked them nicely they would take him back because if that yelling doesn't stop for one minute so you can catch your breath and get hold of an aspirin. . . . No, he won't stop. But go ahead and call your doctor anyway, if you want to. You won't be able to hear anything over the phone, of course, but you will have the reassuring feeling that there is one other human being in the world besides you and this noise-machine.

Don't bother to call your husband. He will only tell you that gosh, maybe there's something wrong with the kid, and you better call the doctor. When you say you've just *called* the doctor he will say well, maybe you better call the doctor again. After you have talked to your husband you can always call your mother. If she is a sensible grandmother—and grandmothers are almost always eminently sensible in this respect—she will have to hang up because she is laughing her head off. This is no comfort. And if she is as sensible a grandmother as all that, she will wait a good twenty-four hours before coming to see you and she will finally come and walk through the front door saying, "Well, did Baby ever stop crying?" Then she will laugh. If she has your mother-in-law with her they will look at each other and laugh.

Meanwhile you will have entered into the O-God-Am-I-Fit-to-Raise-a-Child guilt. This is different from the I-May-Not-Covet-My-Neighbor's-Curls guilt, but similar to the Perhaps-I-Do-Not-Love-Him-As-I-Ought guilt. Basic to all these guilty feelings, of course, is the secret, and accurate, convention that this baby is asking more of you than any human being ought to ask of another, and the complementary feelings that a mother ought to be prepared to give all for her offspring. These two feelings are complementary, but not reconcilable. The mother is damned if she is going to have to take up the slack somehow by kicking herself around a little, and there is absolutely no field that offers such opportunity for guilty self-criticism as bringing up a child.

Guilt about coveting one's neighbor's curls leads naturally to such self-punishing remarks as: "What perfectly magnificent curls little Abercrombie has! I do wish my baby had such lovely hair; tell me—have you checked with your doctor about that wicked squint in Abercrombie's left eye?"

Or, "My husband and I were remarking only yesterday on what lovely curly hair the little fellow has. What a pity he's not a girl!" Abercrombie's mother, riddled by her own doubts, will then thank you politely for your compliments upon the curls, point out that your baby seems so sallow these days—is he getting enough vitamins, do you think?—and you will wheel your carriage in different directions. In five or six years, when your little bruiser hits Abercrombie over the head with a rock, Abercrombie's mother will have more to say about you and your child-raising methods, but by then you will have had more practice in the tigress defending her cubs business, and will have little or no feeling of envy over Abercrombie, that crybaby.

Doubts about being fit to raise a child are best settled before the child is old enough to bring them up himself. Believe me, when he is around fifteen he will have refined this child-torture bit to such an extent that unless you are fully insulated against it, you are going to find that you are being made to reproach yourself for not giving in weak-mindedly to such indulgences as movies on school nights or—if your child psychologist is a girl—wearing high-heeled shoes to school. The truly farsighted baby is the one who learns in his cradle that his mother is going to wonder endlessly about her shortcomings as a parent, and who never allows her to stop wondering for a minute. Prepare your defense: assume from the very first minute that Mother does know best, that no week-old child can dictate to you, that your own solid common sense and proverbial intelligence are enough to carry you through, that from this very minute on, you are never going to reverse a decision once made, and whatever you say, agreeable or not, is going to be final.

Let me know how you come out. For my part, I find myself saying over and over again, "Tomorrow I will do better. Tomorrow I will be patient, no matter what happens. Tomorrow I will not be cross under any provocation. Tomorrow I will start trying to be a model mother." I'll let you know how I come out. Exactly nowhere, that's how I come out. "Tomorrow," I say, "tomorrow I will lay down the law absolutely. I will be reasonable, I will not raise my voice, but I will make it abundantly clear that movies on school nights are . . ."

The worst aspect of all the centuries of tradition and sentiment about mother love and the one hand always reaching out to help, the one face always smiling, the one heart that never loses faith . . . well, the *worst* of it is that it's so easy to think you're falling behind the rest. Certainly you will always leave a light in the window for your wandering boy, but right now someone's got to feed him his strained apricots. You will always be waiting for him, smiling through your tears, glorying in his triumphs, sharing in his defeats, but first you've got to get a dry sheet on his crib. Motherhood is glorious, but it's also one hell of a lot of work, and it's just too easy to get so bogged down in feedings and washings and changings and airings that sometimes days and days go by when you keep forgetting to lift your head and smile proudly through your tears.

There's one very good way to use up any extra guilt you've got left over after being a failure as a mother. Suppose your baby were menaced by a cobra; naturally you would leap in front of the baby and fight off the cobra with your bare hands. Wouldn't you? *Wouldn't* you? It is perfectly possible to reduce yourself to a tearful head-beating wreck over that cobra, because—well, *would* you? Do you love your child enough to awake the few nights that the baby sleeps through his two o'clock bottle? If your husband wakes up and asks what on earth are you doing sitting over there by the window wringing your hands, you be sure to tell him you're wondering if you would have courage enough to save your baby from a cobra. Yes, you tell him that.

Worry, incidentally, is something else again. Worry is when you sit over there by the window all night wringing your hands and picturing *real* dangers, like the probability that Baby will fall out of his crib the minute you are asleep, or the good chance that he will grow up and marry and you will not get along with his wife, or the ever-present perils of mad dogs and those live cartridges that careless people are always leaving around, or smallpox.

Or, if you're still not sleepy, you can just sit there thinking what a miserable wretch you are, the way you treated Baby today when you were so cross. The little sweetheart didn't *mean* to make you unhappy, and even though he kicked the cereal bowl out of your hand *he* didn't know he was doing wrong, and even though no mother would ever punish a tiny baby there is no question that you put him down more abruptly than you would have if you hadn't been angry. The poor little thing can't understand when all of a sudden he looks at his mother whom he trusts and adores above all other human beings and she is scowling and snarling at him and calling him a little beast and the little angel is bewildered and insecure and so he cries and then the mother he had learned to love so dearly almost . . . well, she doesn't *actually* spank him, and anyway those diapers are very thick. But she is very much annoyed. Poor little baby. And he thought his mother loved him. The short-sighted mother will now go tearfully through the darkness to the side of the crib and kiss Baby while he sleeps so exquisitely, and whisper, "Mommy didn't mean it, darling, Mommy's sorry." This almost always wakes the baby, who cries, and before long Mother has completely forgotten that he doesn't really mean it when he tries to drive her crazy.

All my children are prodigies.

—*Yiddish Proverb*

Most of us become parents long before we have stopped being children.

—*Mignon McLaughlin*

When you praise frequently, you are no longer the nagging coach, you are a cheerleader. Who is more inspiring?

—*Cynthia Whitham, M.S.W.*

In every dispute between parent and child, both cannot be right, but they may be, and usually are, both wrong. It is this situation which gives family life its peculiar hysterical charm.

—*Isaac Rosenfeld*

Children are our most valuable natural resource.

—*Herbert Hoover*

Education commences at the mother's knee, and every word spoken within the hearsay of little children tends toward the formation of character.

—*Hosea Ballou*

The Love of Home
by Daniel Webster

It is only shallow-minded pretenders who either make distinguished origin a matter of personal merit, or obscure origin a matter of personal reproach. Taunt and scoffing at the humble conditions of early life affect nobody in America but those who are foolish enough to indulge in them, and they are generally sufficiently punished by public rebuke. A man who is not ashamed of himself need not be ashamed of his early condition.

It did not happen to me to be born in a log cabin; but my elder brothers and sisters were born in a log cabin raised among the snowdrifts of New Hampshire, a period so early that when the smoke first rose from its rude chimney and curled over the frozen hills, there was no similar evidence of a white man's habitation between it and the settlements on the rivers of Canada.

Its remains still exist; I make it an annual visit. I carry my children to it, to teach them the hardships endured by the generations which have gone before them. I love to dwell on the tender recollections, the kindred ties, the early affections and the touching narratives and incidents which mingle with all I know of this primitive family abode.

I weep to think that none of those who inhabited it are now among the living; and if ever I am ashamed of it, or if ever I feel unaffectionate veneration for him who reared it and defended it against savage violence and destruction, cherished all the domestic virtues beneath its roof and, through the fire and blood of a seven years' revolutionary war, shrunk from no danger, no toil, no sacrifice, to serve his country and to raise his children to a condition better than his own, may my name and the name of my posterity be blotted forever from the memory of mankind!

First-generation and recent immigrant parents must be realistic in defining for their children what is right or wrong, good or bad, proper or improper, desirable or undesirable. A recent immigrant mother who insists on raising her daughter in the strict old ways of Mexico may subject her child to embarrassment among other children who are given more freedom to socialize with one another. Likewise, a first-generation father who scolds his teenage son for being assertive and outspoken, in the manner of the new generation of Chicanos, may at the same time be hurting his son's confidence and outlook on life.

—Marcos Behean Hernandez

Reasoning with a child is fine, if you can reach the child's reason without destroying your own.

—John Mason Brown

Youth is a wonderful thing; what a crime to waste it on children.

—George Bernard Shaw

Children are natural mimics. They act like their parents in spite of every effort to teach them good manners.

—Anonymous

It is easier to rule a kingdom than to regulate a family.

—*Japanese Proverb*

Likely as not, the child you can do the least with will do the most to make you proud.

—*Mignon McLaughlin*

We are apt to forget that children watch examples better than they listen to preaching.

—*Roy L. Smith*

The illusions of childhood are necessary experiences: a child should not be denied a balloon because an adult knows that sooner or later it will burst.

—*Marcelene Cox*

A happy childhood is one of the best gifts that parents have in their power to bestow.

—*Irish Proverb*

Changing Behavior:
Attention Is Powerful

by Cynthia Whitham, M.S.W.

We all need and want attention.

Imagine cooking a meal for your family. At the table there is silence. No "Thank you," no "Boy, this smells terrific!" Think how you feel putting extra time in at work, with no acknowledgment from the boss. Picture helping your neighbor and getting no word of gratitude. A day in which we and our efforts are ignored by our spouse, children, friends, neighbors and coworkers is a bleak one.

Children need and want attention, too. Often they seem to have bottomless pits—no amount of attention is enough to satisfy. Your child does not suddenly get enough of your attention and then not want any more. Children's need of attention—adult attention—provides the key to increasing behaviors you like and decreasing behaviors you do not like.

Sometimes it seems as if a child would rather earn negative attention by getting into trouble than *positive* attention for behaving well. It's as if she doesn't know how to do anything else. If your child seems to act up more than cooperate, it could be because she has discovered the quickest way to get your attention is by doing something you dislike.

In the busy lives we lead, we cannot always remember—or find the time—to give full attention to the story she wants to tell, the bug she had found on the grass, or the very bad joke she tells over and over. If our kids do chores without a squawk or play together without bickering, we keep quiet for fear of disturbing the peace. We wouldn't think of interrupting a child reading or playing solitaire to praise her. But if she is mean to her brother, bounces a ball off the ceiling, or uses bad language, we may quickly jump in with a lecture or other punishment. Every time we give more attention to the undesirable behaviors than we give to desirable ones, we are training our children to go for punishment (one form of attention) instead of going for praise (another form of attention).

We can shift the balance. Giving positive attention to behaviors you like encourages your child to do those behaviors more often. The more your child earns positive attention, the less tempting (and necessary) it is to earn punishment.

A child educated only at school is an uneducated child.

—*George Santayana*

Children are the poor's wealth.

—*Danish Proverb*

If a child knows how to work, he is a partial success already.

—*Yiddish Saying*

To make the destruction of a child sure, give him or her unwatched liberty after dark.

—*Anonymous*

There is little use to talk about your child to anyone; other people either have one or haven't.

—*Don Herold*

Telling lies and showing off to get attention are mistakes I made that I don't want my children to make.

—Jane Fonda

Oh, grown-ups cannot understand,
And grown-ups never will
How short the way to fairyland
Across the purple hill.

—Alfred Noyes

Ignorance is a painless evil; so, I should think, is dirt, considering the merry faces that go along with it.

—George Eliot

As parents we hold the stewardship of our children. They are products of heredity, environment, physical body, conscious and subconscious mind. They are experience. They are going in a direction in time and space. And something more: They have the powers of known and unknown. They have the power to affect, use, control and harmonize all of the other powers. And directing their own thoughts, they can control their emotions and ordain their own destiny.

—Author Unknown

Family Shapes

by Mister (Fred) Rogers

The roots of a child's ability to cope and thrive, regardless of circumstance, lie in that child's having had at least a small, safe place (an apartment? a room? a lap?) in which, in the companionship of a loving person, that child could discover that he or she was lovable and capable of loving in return. If a child finds this during the first years of life, he or she can grow up to be a competent, healthy person.

That's why a child's closest caregivers—the people I think of as parents—are very, very special. They are the people who are best able to provide that security, sense of worth and belief that life is worth the effort to live.

It is parents who are special and who help children to grow, not family shapes. The nuclear family, with mother, father and 2.2 children, is perfectly capable of harboring misery, mental illness and violence, and is not necessarily blessed with love, pleasure and resilience, even if it is part of an ideal extended family with aunts, uncles and grandparents all living nearby. Extended family, intact nuclear family, adoptive family, foster family, single-parent family . . . none of these shapes can tell us how the children within them will grow—whether they will thrive or fail. What can tell us a great deal, on the other hand, is the quality of the relationships between the children and the adults within these shapes, particularly those relationships during the first and most formative years of the children's lives.

Children are what we make them.

—*French Proverb*

The joys of parents are secret, and so are their griefs and fears.

—*Sir Francis Bacon*

A child becomes an adult when he realizes that he has a right not only to be right but also to be wrong.

—*Thomas Szasz*

Growing Up

by Anna W. M. Wolf

In the years just before puberty we cannot forget that our sons and daughters are still children. Why else their uncouth manners, their baffling mental absences and those other moments when they suddenly turn to us for help and protection? Now, in adolescence, all this new blossoming and burgeoning, working transformations before our eyes, leaves us breathless. Even the awkwardness of this age takes on special charm, for it is full of promise. Instead of children, it is a young man and a young woman who will be here tomorrow.

Emotionally, these adolescent youngsters are intense and volatile. Intellectually, they may go branching off in all directions, displaying the wild contradictions. At one moment they seem responsibly grown up, at another, unbelievably childish. They are given to bull sessions, theorizing introspection and hifalutin' notions of acceptable behavior, yet often they are unable to perform the necessary tasks under their very noses. For all their moments of startling perceptiveness they may be flagrantly oblivious to other people's feelings. Even when they and their friends seem wholly light-minded, taken up with dates, clothes, gossip and the quest for popularity, they are actually far from sure of themselves. Their surface cockiness conceals their continuous struggle with the questions: Who am I? What will I be good for in the unprotected adult world? Finding no answers, they are frightened . . .

Young people today, whether aware of it or not, are hungry for leadership, readier than they appear to be to respond to a call for effort and sacrifice. On those occasions when they have spoken out, they have made clear that what they miss in their elders is moral conviction, seasoned thought, and — along with a listening ear to rebel voices — an ability to hew to their own lines, knowing why they have chosen a certain course and making clear the reasons for their choice. Then, at least, young people would not feel mired down in a bog of adult uncertainties. With firm foundations, if they still decide to reject their parents' choices, they will at least find something firm and hard and worthy of their mettle to fight against.

Parents: people who bear children and bore teenagers.

—*Eva Shaw*

Much of the fun in talking with kids comes from the startling way they can put a backspin on their answers, saying something that's ridiculous and sensible at the same time. One young nature lover, asked how he would mount a butterfly, replied with devastating logic: "About like a horse if you can get one big enough."

—*Art Linkletter*

When you are dealing with a child, keep all your wits about you, and sit on the floor.

—*Austin O'Malley*

When I was born, I was so surprised I couldn't talk for a year and a half.

—*Gracie Allen*

The Letters of Love

by Swami Shantanand Saraswati

In India, children are not put to bed just because it is eight o'clock. When it is time for the child to go to bed, someone in the family goes to bed with the child. When the child falls asleep, the person leaves the bed. See the feedback given here. When that child grows up, how will he feel toward those parents who were so giving and supportive?

I am reminded of Kabir, who says, "There are many scholars in the world who are constantly studying scriptures, but none of them has become a really wise person. Only that person can become wise who learns two and one half letters. . . ." In Hindi, when we write "prem," which means "love," we use two-and-a-half letters. Kabir is saying that a person only needs to learn the letters of love to become wise. In English, we have four letters, l-o-v-e. How much time do we give to that?

Many of you complain that you were not loved by your parents. There is no sense in complaining about parents. They might not have been given good feedback in their own childhood and were victims of whatever situations they were in. There is something wonderful in being a great parent. Wouldn't you like to be the type of parent about whom your children could feel proud? Then, when you are old and no longer needed, they would still feel that attraction in your presence, as though they were being charmed with Divine energy, love and joy.

If we could change the setting and be wonderful parents, it would be uplifting for us as well as for our younger generation. How much time do we spend with our children? We spend time with television, with girlfriends and boyfriends; we spend time making money. We already have enough abundance, my friends. Now it is time for us to work on our love and selflessness.

Many people love to meditate, to go to seminars and retreats. You are running to a cave and meditating not because you really care for God but because you are still not able to see God in day-to-day life in your puppy, in your spouse, in your child. God is everywhere. God is in me, God is in you. Can you experience God only when you close your eyes?

When you appreciate tenderly, lovingly and joyfully, you not only help others whom you are appreciating and flattering but you help yourself in the process. By making someone happy, you become happy. You may become lost in the beauty of that experience. Ultimately, there is no other mystical experience than being lost.

Give a child enough rope, and he'll trip you up.

—*John Mason Brown*

David had been promised a new puppy for his ninth birthday, but had a tough time choosing among a dozen likely candidates when the family visited the animal shelter.

Finally, he decided upon one nondescript mixed breed . . . one of those that was a little of this and a little of that but with a tail that wouldn't quit wagging.

Telling Mom which puppy he preferred, he rationalized, "I want that one—the one with the happy ending!"

—*Eva Shaw*

It is a delight above all delights to see one's children turn out—as ours have done—all that the heart covets in children; and my delight is so full that I sometimes fancy my heart will have to burst for its own relief.

—*Henry James Sr.*

Parentage is a very important profession; but no test of fitness for it is ever imposed in the interest of the children.

—*George Bernard Shaw*

One word of command from me is obeyed by millions . . . but I cannot get my three daughters, Pamela, Felicity and Joan, to come down to breakfast on time.

— *Viscount Archibald Wavell*

To love playthings well as a child, to lead an adventurous and honorable youth, and to settle when the time arrives, into a green and smiling age, is to be a good artist in life and deserve well of yourself and your neighbor.

— *Robert Louis Stevenson*

A child tells in the street what its father and mother say at home.

— *The Talmud*

The best brought-up children are those who have seen their parents as they are. Hypocrisy is not the parents' first duty.

— *George Bernard Shaw*

Provide Good Models

by Michael Schulman and Eva Mekler

Children learn from observing. If they see you treat people kindly and justly it will confirm for them that you truly value kindness and justice. Many studies show that children become more generous and helpful and adhere to rules more steadfastly after they've seen another child or adult behave that way. Unfortunately, they are also prone to follow bad models. Moreover, if you preach goodness to your child but he sees that you don't practice it . . . he will be more influenced by what you do than by what you say. As he gets older, he's also likely to resent you for being a hypocrite.

Often by simply observing how you behave toward people, your child will understand the moral rule behind your actions. But sometimes it's helpful to put into words what you are doing and why—for example, to explain to her why you are returning a grocery item that was mistakenly placed in your bag, or returning money to a clerk at the supermarket who gave you too much change. If you think about it you'll be surprised at the moral implications of many of your everyday actions that your child witnesses. If she understands the rules guiding your actions, she'll be able to apply them to her own behavior, even though the situations she encounters may be different from yours.

Of a Small Daughter Walking Outdoors

by Frances Frost

Easy, wind!
Go softly here!
She is small
And very dear.

She is young
And cannot say
Words to chase
The wind away.

She is new
To walking, so
Wind, be kind
And gently blow.

On her ruffled head,
On grass and clover.
Easy, wind . . .
She'll tumble over!

When a father gives to his son, both laugh; when a son gives to his father, both cry.

—Yiddish Proverb

The older you get, the faster you ran as a kid.

—Steve Owen

The words a father speaks to his children in the privacy of the home are not overheard at the time, but, as in whispering galleries, they will be clearly heard at the end and by posterity.

—Jean Paul Richter

Years ago when I was first planning Disneyland, I asked one of my teenage daughters what I could add to to the park to make it especially interesting to girls her age. "Boys," she replied, without missing a beat.

—Walt Disney

So long as there is life in the world, each generation will react against its predecessor, correct it, go beyond it. The house that accommodates the fathers never quite suits the children.

—Sir Richard Livingstone

Your Child's Place in a Changing World

by Karyn Feiden

Raising a responsible child is a highly complex task, but most parents do find that they are successful at it. The key is to assemble the building blocks. A child with a strong sense of self-esteem, the capacity to empathize, an understanding of the differences between right and wrong, confidence in her own judgment and a grasp of the consequences of her actions has the best chance to flower into responsible adulthood.

Chances are that if parents model appropriate behavior, their child will eventually learn to imitate it. But parents should not feel guilty or anxious when they make a mistake. Even if they know, in theory, that it is better to provide constructive feedback than to criticize angrily, parents will lose their temper at times. If parents acknowledge their slip-ups and use them as a tool to let their child know it is normal to make mistakes, they will have taught another enduring lesson.

Parents need to define their notion of responsibility broadly. While loyalty to friends and family and commitment to their jobs are necessary parts of the package, parents should not restrict their child's vision of the world to their own. A child who is raised responsibly will find her own vision, and it will be one that empowers her, enables her and gives her hope.

Definition of a child: something that stands halfway between an adult and the TV screen.

—*Anonymous*

There's nothing wrong with teenagers that telling them won't aggravate.

—*J. B. Priestley*

Oh, to be only half as wonderful as my child thought I was when he was small, and only half as stupid as my teenager now thinks I am.

—*Rebecca Richards*

One must have the courage to educate children; it is their future . . . not ours.

—*Anonymous*

When children appear, we justify all our weaknesses, compromises, snobberies, by saying: "It's for the children's sake."

—*Anton Chekhov*

We fear something before we hate it; a child who fears noises becomes a man who hates noise.

— *Cyril Connolly*

A child responds so readily to guidance when it is lovingly given — she catches a thought or suggestion so quickly, weaving into it the fabric of living so eagerly, turning so trustingly to those who have seen and understood and helped, showing so surely the confidence and security and understanding, that one rejoices in doing all one can to help the child find the ways to make a living thing of joy and beauty and usefulness.

— *Grace Langdon, Ph.D.*

A child is a person who is often spoiled because you can't spank the two sets of grandparents.

— *Eva Shaw*

The closest friends I have made all through life have been people who also grew up close to a loved and loving grandmother or grandfather.

— *Margaret Mead*

Daddies

by Edgar A. Guest

I would rather be the daddy
Of a romping, roguish crew,
Of a bright-eyed chubby laddie
And a little girl or two,
Than a monarch of a nation
In his high and lofty seat,
Taking empty adoration
From the subjects at his feet.

I would rather own their kisses
As at night to me they run,
Than to be the king who misses
All the simpler forms of fun.
When his dreary day is ending
He is dismally alone,
But when my sun is descending
There are joys for me to own.

He may ride to horns and drumming;
I must walk a quiet street,
But when once they see me coming
Then on joyous, flying feet,
They come racing to me madly
And I catch them with a swing

And I say it proudly, gladly,
That I'm happier than a king.

You may talk of lofty places,
You may boast of pomp and power,
Men may turn their eager faces
To the glory of an hour,
But give the humble station
With its joys that long survive,
For the daddies of the nation
Are the happiest men alive.

There's a lot more to being a woman than being a mother, but there's a hell of a lot more to being a mother than most people suspect.

—*Roseanne*

How can one say no to a child? How can one be anything but a slave to one's own flesh and blood?

—*Henry Miller*

Babies do not want to hear about babies; they like to be told of giants and castles.

—*Samuel Johnson*

A child should always say what's true,
And speak when he is spoken to,
And behave mannerly at table:
At least as far as he is able.

—*Robert Louis Stevenson*

A Little Peach in the Orchard Grew

by Lucile Hadley

All I had to do, said the magazine quiz, was to answer the questions truthfully and spontaneously, add up my score, and turn to page 105. On page 105 would be the grand unveiling: was I the Mother Type or was I the Wife Type?

To me, this seemed to offer a very narrow range of possibilities. What if, under my housewifely exterior, I was really the Harem Type or the Gun Moll Type or the Helen of Troy Type? None of these was very likely but, still, I resented the stuffy limitations set by this Dr. Albert O'Whoosis who had concocted the quiz. Dr. Albert O'Whoosis, not realizing that I had once been hailed as the Peach Type, was under-estimating my more lush possibilities.

Back in South Bend Central High School, in the school *Interlude,* they printed "A little peach in the orchard grew" under my graduation picture and this, I would have you know, was a triumph of no mean scope. Lots of the other girls had to be content with noncommittal and lackluster sentiments like "Who shall find a valiant woman!" or "Prithee! Hark! A maid doth enter," or "Her voice was ever gentle, soft, and low, an excellent thing in woman."

At the age of seventeen, none of us gave a hoot about being soft-spoken or valiant women but "peach" . . . well, now, *there* you had something. Something more on the Clara Bow order. I distinctly remember that none of the more laudable honors that came my way (making the varsity volleyball team and winning a debate about the Panama Canal) carried the full fruity flavor of my *Interlude* analysis. Even today, whenever I open a tin of canned peaches, I always read the label (Grade A . . . hand-picked . . . packed in regulation heavy syrup) with a certain proud nostalgia. Yes, sir!

You can readily understand, therefore, why the proposed stakes in this magazine quiz hurt my feelings. Why, this upstart of a professor wasn't even giving me a *chance* to see if I had the makings of anything interesting. Just Wife Type or Mother Type, he said. MOREOVER, even meeting him on his own niggardly terms, where did he get this either/or stuff? What, pray, was to prevent me from being a perfectly peachy blend of *both?* Who, pray, was to say that Miss Peach of 1927 couldn't jolly well be Mrs. Peach of 1949?

Not Dr. O'Whoosis, by a long shot. I guess I could show him a thing or two with one arm tied behind me. I'd pile up a score that would make him sit up and whistle.

The questions were awfully easy. It was no strain at all to be truthful and spontaneous. The professor asked silly, easy things like: "If you had an extra five dollars, what would you buy? A new hat for yourself or one for your child?" With only a faint sneer as to what kind of a hat I'd find for five bucks nowadays, I passed on to the next one: "Would you rather curl up with a good novel or read Mother Goose aloud to the baby?" I settled that one in record time and sailed into the next bit of soul-searching: "Are you able (was I able!!) to enjoy an evening out with your husband or do you fret about the children at home?" And the question about whether or not my husband ever had to get his own breakfast made me laugh out loud. Naturally, my husband got his own breakfast. You don't expect a grown man to go to work on an empty stomach, do you?

Well, as I say, the questions were a pip. So was my score. I barely made the grade as a wife and I failed—utterly, dismally—as a mother. Which just goes to show that being analyzed as a peach doesn't guarantee a blamed thing. I think the only reason I skinned through as a wife was because I said I could enjoy a carefree evening out with my husband. This, of course, scored heavily against me as a mother but . . . oh, well, some days you can't make a nickel. But, even allowing for the law of averages, there was no excuse for anyone (outside of Dracula or Frankenstein) to flunk motherhood with a score like mine.

"Your score of .008 reveals," announced Dr. O'Whoosis, like the crack of doom, on page 105, "that you have no Mother Instinct."

This was a fine how-do-you-do. They let you go ahead and bear three children and then tell you you're not the type. Offhand, I didn't know whether I was supposed to go out and quietly slit my own throat or else drown the three children in the bathtub. Clearly, someone had to get out of the way.

As I tossed on my sleepless cot that night, I tried to cheer myself up by thinking that, at any rate, my children had an *honest* mother. I could have, you know, said I was crazy about reading Mother Goose aloud and no one would have been wiser. And that hypothetical five bucks I spent on a hat for myself . . . well, gee, maybe I shouldn't have done it but I honestly thought Susie's red felt would get through another winter. Mine was a sight.

I also made medical excuses for myself. I decided, somewhat bittterly, that the Mother Instinct was probably lacking because my three children had all been Caesarean births. There was probably something about having labor pains that turned the trick. Just three days of gas pains didn't count.

With the dawn, though, I began to feel better about Mother Goose and the hat and the gas pains. It explained, for example, why I have always wanted to snarl and bite at baby photographers. Small wonder. No Mother Instinct to make me joyously respond to their gurgling drivel. ("What a beautiful, beautiful child you have there, Mother. Gitchee-goo, Baby, gitchee-goo, Mother. By the way, you'll want at least three gross of these oil-tinted miniatures, won't you, Mother?")

I always thought (somewhat abased) that I wanted to bite photographers because I had a deficiency of calcium or something in my system. I once read about a woman on a low-calcium diet who had an irresistible urge to bite the shoulder of a certain laundry man. The doctor advised her husband to talk the laundry man into letting her do it. Bad things, repressions.

Now I saw no particular good reason as to why I, with no Mother Instinct to hold me back, couldn't let loose and sink my teeth into the very next photographer who gurgled at me. Come to think about it, there were lots of other people I wouldn't mind biting, either. Such as all electrical guitars, tap dancing, baton twirling, and elocution teachers who want to groom my children for MGM, Carnegie Hall, or the Palladium.

Of course, these talent scouts don't start heckling you until the baby is around a year old (I understand they have miniature electrical guitars, infant size) but the ordinary commercial salesmen are on hand from birth on. Yes, I think that . . . after the photographers and talent scouts . . . I will most enjoy biting salesmen. (Naturally, I intend—thanks to Dr. O'Whoosis—to be an emancipated woman from now on. No more of this secret life of Walter Mitty stuff, just *dreaming* about biting.)

I'm sharpening my fangs for those salesmen who—if you resist their product—make you feel like a monster that eats its young. "You mean," they sneer, "that you intend to go through life without having your child's first shoes immortalized as bronze bookends? You mean you're going to make your baby eat out of a spoon that doesn't have the same design as your own Community Plate? Ugh."

Ah, how it all comes back to me. Everyone told me that my third baby would be Pure Joy ("You won't worry, you'll just enjoy him," they said), but they weren't reckoning on the commercial snakes in my Eden.

I distinctly remember the day I left the maternity ward, two years ago. With my bundle of Pure Joy in my arms, I sat there in a wheelchair waiting for the elevator. Homeward bound. My husband stood beside me, loaded with two pots of hydrangeas, a baby blanket and my suitcase. Suddenly, a nurse raced frantically down the hall.

"Oh," she exclaimed loudly, so everyone could hear, "don't you want Baby's little identification bracelet as a souvenir?" Thanking her for her thoughtfulness, I awkwardly shifted the baby and pocketed a two-inch bead bracelet that spelled out "H-a-s-l-e-y." Then to my horror, I heard her say briskly, "And that'll be one dollar, please."

So, my husband put down the two pots of hydrangeas, the baby blanket and the suitcase, and dragged out his wallet. It wasn't so much that it left us with just two bus tokens to get home on, understand, but the principle of the thing. With a hospital bill that would choke a horse, couldn't they have tossed that five-cent bracelet in for free? A little nosegay to my motherhood? No.

One week home from the hospital, the insurance salesman showed up. Like all loving and far-sighted mothers, I wanted . . . didn't I . . . to prepare for baby's college education? I did, but I also thought it would be sort of nice if we first paid for the baby himself. I'd never forgive myself if the finance company came and took Danny away as they did my ironer.

By the time the Elite Studio called, my disposition was getting a little frayed around the edges.

"Is this Mrs. Louis Hasley?" the voice caroled brightly. *"Congratulations!* You have just won a contest! Your name has been selected to receive an 8 x 10 tinted picture of your new baby! When would like your appointment?"

For a split second, I thought motherhood was going to pay off. I thought I was really going to get something for nothing, but then the bright voice caroled that—whereas the picture was free—obviously there would be a charge for the solid gold frame that went with it. Oh, obviously.

I had about lost my faith in human nature when the Welcome Wagon rolled up to my front curbing. The Welcome Wagon lady had a market basket full of FREE gifts (all right, *be* crude and call them advertising samples) for me and my babe, all donated by local businessmen. This touched me to the quick. Just think! Those busy, busy tycoons taking time to select gifts personally for poor little me. With tears smarting my eyes, I started to relieve the woman of her basket but she wouldn't let go.

It seemed that there was a little ceremony that went with the presentation and I, crude that I was, was rushing the deal. Each little gift, I learned the hard way, was to be slowly and impressively lifted out—accompanied by a sales talk. My part in the ritual (and believe me, all we lacked was some background organ music) was to utter a little cluck of joy and gratitude when she finally handed it over.

I also had to remember directions. For instance, as I received a quart of homogenized milk I was told that the milkman would be around the next morning to collect the empty bottle. He was also very anxious to see how I enjoyed the way the fatty particles were all broken down and how I appreciated the 400 U.S.P. vitamin D units from irradiated ergosterol. Would I have my report ready, please, when he came? (About 6:45 A.M.)

Well, it was a bit of a nuisance to swill down the whole quart of milk that evening and prepare my testimonial but . . . there, there, I'm talking like an ingrate. The gifts *were* free and the entire ceremony only took about one and a half hours. I *was* grateful but I decided, just the same, to ask my husband to build a moat around the house to discourage further callers. The after-care of new mothers (I read somewhere) included rest and freedom from anxiety and pressing decision.

He didn't get the moat built in time, though, to ward off Miss Pinkle, a Super Marvel Book Salesman. Miss Hattie Pinkle, a retired schoolteacher, caught me with my guard down because I'd caught a bad head cold (lack of rest) and didn't want to stand in the open door.

Unwittingly, I invited her to step inside, but as soon as I discovered her mission in life, I began to sneeze and hack — in careless fashion — into my Kleenex. I even mentioned that tuberculosis ran rampant on my mother's side of the family, but Miss Pinkle, as I learned to my sorrow, was made of stern stuff. She not only settled down on the davenport but bade me cuddle close to her so that we could look at the Super Marvel Book pictures together.

And beautiful pictures they were, too. Not to mention the valuable and illuminating printed material that went along with them. Did I know what caused lightning? Did I know the different kinds of cloud formation? Could I explain radioactivity? Did I know what makes moss grow on the north side of trees? Could I even explain a rainbow?

No. How then, asked Miss Pinkle (closing in for the kill), was I going to explain it all to my wee one when he asked me?

How, indeed? Wee one's father wasn't any help as Nature Boy; he just specialized in Victorian poetry at Notre Dame. But sitting there bleary-eyed and with a tub of diapers awaiting me in the basement, I couldn't quite get into the spirit of the thing. If I furnished my wee one with dry pants, wasn't that enough? Did he have to complicate things by asking about lightning? But I knew, deep down inside of me, that I was being an unimaginative dolt about the whole affair. Making rapid calculations, I figured that we could (by just living on rice) probably finish paying the last installments of the book by 1964.

Then a horrible thought struck me. If my wee one never asked what made lightning (and I wasn't going to bring it up), why . . . why, it would just mean our life savings would go down the drain. Not to mention getting beriberi from the steady rice diet.

Wouldn't it be far more sensible never to let my wee one see lightning? Lock him in a closet every time it stormed? Or (and this was more constructive), why not give wee one a piece of string and a key and push him out in the storm to discover and harness lightning for himself? After all, no one made things easy for Benjamin Franklin.

So I said, out loud: "No one made it easy for B. Franklin."

Miss Pinkle looked so dazed that, warming to my theme, I launched into the rugged boyhoods of Franklin, the Wright Brothers, Robert Fulton, Marconi and Edison. Did they have the Super Marvel Books? Not on your life. Triumphantly, I pointed out that to have such books within easy reach would soften a lad's moral fiber, quench the spark for research, stunt his ingenuity, dull his boyish curiosity at God's natural wonders . . .

Well, I put in a hard morning's work but Miss Pinkle finally slunk out the front door: dazed, converted, apologetic. The last I heard of her she had given up her shady traffic in worthwhile books and was selling ladies' ready-to-wear in Penney's basement. So I guess I outwitted Miss Pinkle, all right, but look at the time and energy I had to expend in order to save face. If I had only known then what I know now—to wit, no Mother Instinct, like an albatross around my neck—I could just have laughed in Miss Pinkle's face.

"Ha," I could have laughed in Miss Pinkle's face, "so you think I'm interested in my own children, eh? Make tracks, Pinkle."

Well, you can see for yourself just how indebted I am to Dr. Albert O'Whoosis for this new freedom. (You can also see for yourself just what the years have done to the little peach in the orchard growing but let's skip lightly over that, shall we?) Actually, I can hardly wait for him to bring out another quiz and let me find out some more about myself.

It is vital for adults to recognize that children are complete, complex human beings with the same sensitivities and requirements for emotional support as adults. Indeed, at one extreme, researchers on child abuse suggest that it is our ability to distance ourselves from our children that allows us to hurt them.

—*Edward Zigler, Ph.D.*

Having a baby is better than winning an Olympic gold medal.

—*Mary Lou Retton*

Don't gossip about the children of others while yours are still growing up.

—*Jewish Saying*

If a child tells a lie, tell him that he has told a lie, but don't call him a liar. If you define him as a liar, you break down his confidence in his own character.

—*Jean Paul Richter*

No one ever keeps a secret so well as a child.

—*Victor Hugo*

Kids Still Say the Darndest Things
by Art Linkletter

At one point on *Art Linkletter's House Party* program [the long-running, nationally popular, *live* television show hosted in the 1950s by Linkletter], I offered to give an autographed copy of *Kids Say the Darndest Things* to any viewer who would send in a kid's saying bright enough or funny enough to be used on the air. The result was a flood of mail that is still coming in. Here, highly condensed, are just a few of these gems:

Five-year-old: "I've got the smartest dog. All I have to say is, 'Are you coming in or aren't you?' and he either comes in or he doesn't."

Three-year-old, sadly, on being told she had her shoes on the wrong feet: "But, Mommy, these are the only feet I have."

Six-year-old, hopefully, on being told there would be no school because of George Washington's birthday: "Can I go to George's party?"

Five-year-old, on being given her allowance: "Oh, I just *love* to hold this money; it makes my hand feel so good!"

Four-year-old in church for the first time, as the usher approaches with the collection plate: "Don't pay for me, Daddy. I'm under five."

Four-year-old, bursting into tears at the dinner table: "My teeth just stepped on my tongue."

Wide-eyed little boy in a restaurant; his mother has just asked the waiter for the leftover steak to take home to the dog: "Oh, boy! At last! We're gonna get a dog!"

Dialogue between mother and five-year-old who's in the next room:
"Mommy, can I eat this candy I found on the floor?"
"No, there are germs on it."
Slight pause.
"Mommy, can I eat it now? I licked all the germs off."

Home and the Baby

by Edgar A. Guest

Home was never home before,
Till the baby came.
Love no golden jewels wore,
Till the baby came.
There was joy, but now it seems
Dreams were not the rosy dreams,
Sunbeams not such golden beams —
Till the baby came.

Home was never really gay,
Till the baby came.
I'd forgotten how to play,
Till the baby came.
Smiles were never half so bright,
Troubles never half so light,
Worry never took to flight,
Till the baby came.

Home was never half so blest,
Till the baby came.
Lacking something that was the best,
Till the baby came.
Kisses were not half so sweet,
Love not really so complete,
Joy had never found our street
Till the baby came.

Essay on a Son
by Alan Beck

A boy is a magical creature—you can lock him out of your workshop, but you can't lock him out of your heart. You can get him out of your study, but you can't get him out of your mind.

Might as well give up—he is your captor, your jailer, your boss and your master—a freckled-faced, pint-sized, cat-chasing bundle of noise. But when you come home at night with only the shattered pieces of your hopes and dreams, he can mend them like new with two magic words—"Hi, Dad!"

Essay on a Daughter
by Alan Beck

Little girls are the nicest things that happen to people. They are born with a little bit of angelshine about them, and though it wears thin sometimes there is always enough left to lasso your heart—even when they are sitting in the mud, or crying temperamental tears, or parading up the streets in Mother's best clothes.

The child sees everything which has to be experienced and learned as a doorway. So does the adult. But what to the child is an entrance is to the adult only a passage.

—Friedrich Wilhelm Nietzsche

Children aren't happy with nothing to ignore, And that's what parents were created for.

—Odgen Nash

Parenthood: The state of being better chaperoned than you were before marriage.

—Marcelene Cox

Over the years I have learned that motherhood is much like an austere religious order, the joining of which obligates one to relinquish all claims to personal possessions.

—Nancy Stahl

Unlike grown-ups, children have little need to deceive themselves.

—Goethe

Twenty-Five Sermons
by Jeremy Taylor (c. 1653)

No man can tell but he that loves his children, how many delicious accents make a man's heart dance in the pretty conversations of those dear pledges; their childishness, their stammering, their little angers, their innocence, their imperfections, their necessities are so many little emanations of joy and comfort to him that delights in their persons and society; but he that loves not his wife and children, feeds a lioness at home and broods a nest of sorrow.

A girl of fifteen generally has a greater number of secrets than an old man.

—*José Ortega y Gasset*

We have not passed that subtle line between childhood and adulthood until we move from the passive voice to the active voice—this is, until we have stopped saying, "It got lost," and say, "I lost it."

—*Sydney J. Harris*

Unless you are the victim, nothing is quite so funny as kids mimicking their elders.

—*Eva Shaw*

Women make us poets, children make us philosophers.

—*Malcolm de Chazal*

It's not easy being a mother. If it were, fathers would do it.

—*Dorothy*, The Golden Girls

I know how to do anything—I'm a mom.

—*Roseanne*

A Letter to His Son

by Charles Dickens

My Dearest Plorn,

I write this note today because your going away is much upon my mind, and because I want you to have a few parting words from me to think of now and then at quiet times. I need not tell you that I love you dearly, and am very, very sorry in my heart to part with you. But this life is half made up of partings, and these pains must be borne. It is my comfort and sincere conviction that you are going to try the life for which you are best fitted. I think its freedom and wildness more suited to you than any experiment in study or office would ever have been; and without that training, you could have followed no other suitable occupation.

What you have already wanted until now has been a set, steady, constant purpose. I therefore exhort you to persevere in a thorough determination to do whatever you have to do as well as you can do it. I was not so old as you are now when I first had to win my food, and to do this out of determination, and I have never slackened in it since.

Never take a mean advantage of anyone in any transaction, and never be hard upon people who are in your power. Try to do to others, as you would have them do to you, and do not be discouraged if they fail sometimes. It is much better for you that they should fail in obeying the greatest rule laid down by your Saviour, than that you should.

I put a New Testament among your books, for the very same reason, and with the very same hopes that made me write an easy account of it for you, when you were a little child; because it is the best book that ever was or ever will be known to the world, and because it teaches you the best lessons by which any human creature who tries to be truthful and faithful to duty can possibly be guided. As your brothers have gone away, one by one, I have written to each such words as I am now writing to you, and entreated them all to guide themselves by this book, putting aside the interpretations and inventions of men.

You will remember that you have never at home been wearied about religious observances or mere formalities. I have always been anxious not to weary my children with such things before they are old enough to form opinions respecting them. You will therefore understand the better that I now must solemnly impress upon you the truth and beauty of the Christian religion, as it came from Christ himself, and the impossibility of your going far wrong if you humbly but heartily respect it.

Only one thing more in this head. The more we are in earnest as to feeling it, the less we are disposed to hold forth about it. Never abandon the wholesome practice of saying your own private prayers, night and morning. I have never abandoned it myself, and I know the comfort of it.

I hope you will always be able to say in afterlife, that you had a kind father. You cannot show your affection for him so well, or make him so happy, as by doing your duty.

Your affectionate father

What is more enchanting than the voices of young people when you can't hear what they say?

—*L. P. Smith*

One of the signs of passing youth is the birth of the sense of fellowship with other human beings as we take our place among them.

—*Virginia Woolf*

A mother snatched up the toddler after he'd broken a lamp, smeared jelly on the cat and applied makeup all over his face—and all that before morning nap time. Scrubbing off the last of the Pink Passion lipstick, she was heard saying, "That settles it! You're going to be an only child!"

—*Eva Shaw*

Young people are always more given to admiring what is gigantic than what is reasonable.

—*Eugene Delacroix*

If a child is to keep alive his inborn sense of wonder, he needs the companionship of at least one adult who can share it, rediscovering with him the joy, excitement and mystery of the world we live in.

—Rachel Carson

Children despise their parents until the age of forty, when they suddenly become just like them—thus preserving the system.

—Quentin Crewe

Grown-ups never understand anything for themselves, and it is tiresome for children to be always and forever explaining things to them.

—Antoine de Saint-Exupéry

For those who believe in God no explanation is needed; for those who do not believe in God no explanation is possible.

—Father John LaFarge

Raising Good Kids in a World That's Not

by Paul Vitello and Carol Polsky

A funny thing happened on the way from our first Lamaze class to now.

We are the parents of a four-year-old and a one-year-old. We have passed through the happy gauntlet of keeping the kids fed, clothed, doctored, dolled, nuzzled, played with, spoken to, listened to and, to the extent that we could, untroubled by the complexities of the world.

Now we find ourselves at the entrance to a new and trickier path.

It would be hard to put a finger on exactly when it appeared. It was somewhere around the time our son asked us why robbers rob, why people die, and why some people are poor and some people are rich. We have no idea where he got these dark questions: snatches of conversation overheard, pieces of news footage on TV. But it brought home for us the fact that he was no longer in the cocoon of babyhood. He had entered the world, for better or worse. And we had some explaining to do.

What should we say? How much do you tell a child? I know these are questions with flexible answers: You tell them as much as they can understand; as much as you know. But in grappling with those first tricky pop quizzes on life and death, fair and unfair, right and wrong, we realized that what we were up against was bigger than the questions themselves.

We were beginning to grapple with The Big Question of parenting: how to raise good kids in a world that is not always good. Not just well-mannered kids, but kids who will be honest, kind and open-minded. Kids who are trustworthy. Kids with a sense of purpose, with convictions and the courage to stand by them.

Our guess is that some great kids come from great homes, and some from less-than-great circumstances. As with anything at the high end of the human spectrum, there is a certain mystery about these things.

But it seemed likely that the odds would improve by paying attention to the process. So we have begun to do that. And here are a number of ideas we've picked up so far. They come from a wide array of parents, including professionals in the field of developmental behavior, along with just regular moms and dads with good kids. We think of this as a working list, and we expect it will grow as the kids do.

Set a positive example. Everybody we talked to said this in one way or another. Vincent Guarnaccia, Ph.D., associate professor of psychology at Hofstra University on Long Island, put it best: "Children become civilized by living in a civilized environment. That's one where there is a relaxed acceptance of people, where husbands and wives relate to each other, where everybody could be doing his or her own thing under the same roof, but are still connected."

Listen to your kids. Just about everybody said this, too. Don't be so intent on managing them that you don't enjoy the spontaneity of just being with them. Let them talk, give them the attention you would give your best friend.

Talk about good values in explicit ways. Preaching honesty or loyalty is not necessarily as good as praising it when you see it demonstrated by your child or someone else.

Remember: They're watching. If you don't want the kids to lie and cheat, don't lie and cheat. "I would go so far as to say that this means obeying the speed limit, and not bringing home pencils or paper that belong to your employer," says Kermit Little, a psychologist at Texas Tech University and a father of nine. "It means not asking the children to tell callers that you are not home when you are."

Be united in parenting. Since kids learn almost everything by example, this is one of the ways they learn the art of collaboration.

Speak their language. Not baby talk, but the language that has meaning for your child. "Saying 'I love you' a million times a day is not necessarily enough," says Wally Goodard, Ph.D., assistant professor of family and child development at Auburn University in Auburn, Alabama. "Some kids just need you to sit on the sofa next to them while they do their homework. Another kid might want you to go shopping with her. You have to communicate in ways that are valued and understood by that child."

Be specific with your praise. Instead of just saying "Good job!" say, "That's great how you put those blocks away, and put those puzzle pieces in the box," or "I really liked how you made Joey feel better by saying that." It helps for a young child to learn what he's doing right.

Help develop social skills. Put as much effort into it as you do in helping your children with their homework.

Studies show that the teenagers most at risk for behavior problems, including depression and dropping out of school, are those with the poorest social skills.

Joseph Price, Ph.D., a psychology professor at San Diego State University, thinks children's friendships should be as high a parental priority as academic success. He suggests using role playing and making gentle, specific suggestions to help kids learn. Teach them to be assertive without being aggressive. "Assertive sometimes means having to plow into the catcher covering home plate," he explains. "It does not mean punching him in the nose." Also suggest to them that humor is often the best way around obstructions.

Teach them about choosing friends. Dr. Price suggests reinforcing good friendships with specific praise: "I like the way Annie showed her concern by coming over to see how you were after you fell in the playground."

Teach the importance of trust. Kids should learn by your example that a promise is a promise. "This is at the heart of teaching the basic character values such as honesty, loyalty and consideration of others," says Michael Obsatz, Ph.D., associate professor of sociology at Macalester College in St. Paul. "Kids have to be shown what it means to be consistent, what it means to do what we say we're going to do."

Treat your children with respect. They'll be more likely to treat others the same way. Call them names and belittle them, and they'll be more likely to do that, too.

Volunteer. Bring the kids along. Get involved in the community, the schools, in your neighborhood. Children learn about principles and putting personal convictions on the line by watching others do it.

Let them learn from their mistakes. Help them to face adverse situations, but do not always shield children from them. "Strength of character is developed through experience, and the wise parent will provide opportunities where they're more likely to succeed," says Professor Goddard.

Try to avoid power struggles. Help young kids perform tasks by offering to assist them and making a game of it. Say, "You pick up the yellow pieces and I'll pick up the green ones." Suggest something fun to do after the task is completed. Give children a sense of control and some choices, too: Does your daughter want to wear the red shirt or the plaid? Does she want to keep all the trucks together or would she rather park them with the cars?

Teach your kids not to be ashamed of walking away from a fight. Boys, especially, have trouble with this, says Professor Obsatz. "Society teaches boys to suppress every emotion except anger. Anger is the only acceptable emotion." So besides helping young men learn to express the whole gamut of their emotions, he says, "It is very important to help them understand the need to manage one's anger and the difference between feelings and actions."

Don't be afraid to be a parent. Set limits. Enforce them with clear expectations and clear consequences. But make sure there aren't so many rules that your children have trouble following them.

Encourage your kids to cut themselves some slack. If it takes a number of tries to get something done, so be it. "Children should be familiar with the concept of 'process'," says Professor Obsatz. "That things develop, and that if things are not the way we want them now, we can work toward making them better."

Give them space to grow and discover. With all the emphasis here on how to raise them, we don't mean to overlook the mysterious and wonderful process by which kids raise themselves, too. Let them explore on their own, think on their own, make their own pleasures in life, unconcerned with applause or disapproval from the audience that is us, their parents.

There they are, our Golden Rules as we know them. And aside from all the neat tips we picked up, we learned that when people talked about their kids they were almost always thoughtful, serious, uncompromising, funny, high-minded, wistful, generous, forgiving, committed, moral, friendly and willing to talk long into the night to strangers asking earnest questions. In other words, they were the type of people we would like our kids to become.

It is only with the heart that one can see rightly; what is essential is invisible to the eye.

—*Antoine de Saint-Exupéry*

God could not be everywhere and therefore he made mothers.

—*Jewish Proverb*

Family quarrels are bitter things. They don't go according to any rules. They're not like aches or wounds, they're more like splits in the skin that won't heal because there's not enough material.

—*F. Scott Fitzgerald*

The greatest thing in family life is to take a hint when a hint is intended—and not to take a hint when a hint is not intended.

—*Robert Frost*

Definition of a teenager: people of a certain age who express a burning desire to be different by dressing exactly alike.

—*Eva Shaw*

If you bungle raising your children, I don't think whatever else you do well matters very much.

—Jacqueline Kennedy Onassis

There are times when parenthood seems nothing but feeding the mouth that bites you.

—Peter de Vries

What harsh judges fathers are to all young men!

—Terrence (c. 190-159 B.C.)

The beauty of "spacing" children many years apart lies in the fact that parents have time to learn the mistakes that were made with the older ones—which permits them to make exactly the opposite mistakes with the younger ones.

—Sydney J. Harris

Misery is when grown-ups don't realize how miserable kids can feel.

—Suzanne Heller

In youth we learn, in age we understand.

—Marie von Ebner-Eschenbach

The popular idea that a child forgets easily is not an accurate one. Many people go right through life in the grip of an idea which has been impressed on them in very tender years.

—Agatha Christie

Your grandchild will not care if you live on a very restricted budget, believe me. Grandma is warm, cozy and loving, and she always has time. To the child, that is what is important. Even if you do not live near your grandchild— even if you make your home in some distant part of the country—you can be warm, close and loving. You can set aside special times for sharing with your grandchild. And that is the greatest gift of all.

—Lanie Carter

A boy becomes an adult three years before his parents think he does, and about two years after he thinks he does.

—Lewis B. Hershey

Nowadays, parents take a "problem" child to a psychiatrist to talk through difficulties. Granddad used the do-it-yourself method and took the kid fishing.

—Eva Shaw

To maintain a joyful family requires much from both the parents and the children. Each member of the family has to become, in a special way, the servant of the others.

—Pope John Paul II

The most painful death in all the world is the death of a child. When a child dies, when one child dies—not the eleven per one thousand we talk about statistically, but the one that a mother held briefly in her arms—he leaves an empty place in a parent's heart that will never heal.

—Thomas H. Kean

Childhood smells of perfume and brownies.

—David Leavitt

Where does discipline end? Where does cruelty begin? Somewhere between these, thousands of children inhabit a voiceless hell.

—François Mauriac

Never Scare a Child

by Henry Miller

Never scare a child by threats. "Look out or the boogeyman will get you." "Be good or the ragpicker will put you in his bag and carry you away." "Do what I say or I'll beat you within an inch of your life." "If you don't behave you will go to hell and burn for millions of years."

These damnable, destructive, fear-suggestions have done more to warp, cripple and curse human life than all other factors combined.

Character is never matured through fear, only through reason.

As we read the school report on our children, we realize a sense of relief that can rise to delight that—thank heaven—nobody is reporting in this fashion on us.

—*J. B. Priestley*

Age seventeen is the point in the journey when the parents retire to the observation car; it is the time when you stop being critical of your eldest son and he starts being critical of you.

—*Sally and James Reston*

All the time a person is a child, he is both a child and learning to be a parent. After he becomes a parent he becomes predominantly a parent reliving childhood.

—*Dr. Benjamin Spock*

The Old-Time Family

by Edgar A. Guest

It makes me smile to hear 'em tell
each other nowadays
The burdens they are bearing, with
a child or two to raise.
Of course the cost of living has
gone soaring to the sky
And our kids are wearing garments that
my parents couldn't buy.
Now my father wasn't wealthy, but I
never heard him squeal
Because eight of us were sitting at
the table every meal.

People fancy they are martyrs if their
children number three,
And four or five they reckon makes
a large-sized family.
A dozen hungry youngsters at a table I have seen
And their daddy didn't grumble when they
licked the platter clean.
Oh, I wonder how these mothers and
these fathers up-to-date
Would like the job of buying little
shoes for seven or eight.

We were eight around the table in those
happy days back then,
Eight that cleaned out plates of pot-pot
and then passed them up again;
And with mightily little money in
the purse, as I have said,
But with all the care we brought them, and
through all the days of stress,
I never heard my father or my
mother wish for less.

Cleaning your house while your children are still growing is like shoveling the walk before it stops snowing.

—Phyllis Diller

You can sort of be married, you can sort of be divorced, you can sort of be living together, but you can't sort of have a baby.

—David Shire

As a grandfather, I'm entitled to a few words of sage advice to the young: I would spend more time with my children.

—John Huston

A Letter to My Chosen Child
by Alice Ross

My Dearest Daughter:
We are about to mark the fourth anniversary of your arrival in our home. Sometimes I think about the circuitous route Daddy and I traveled before finding you, and my heart skips a beat. It would have been so easy for us to miss you.

Before you came to us, we had worked for seven years to become a family but had succeeded only in adding our names to various adoption agency waiting lists. One of our most constructive moves was telling everyone we knew about our desire to adopt because, in doing so, we found you.

About five years ago, our friends Genie and Ron adopted a baby. In the midst of our own adoption quest, we relied heavily on our experienced friends for information and moral support. They introduced us to a network of enthusiastic adoptive parents who promised to help us. One evening Genie called with a lead on a baby girl from another country who was in foster care and who would soon be available for adoption. We immediately contacted the Department of Social Services and were thrilled to be invited to meet with a social worker.

The meeting went well. Daddy and I listened eagerly as the social worker described the child she was hoping to place as a happy, intelligent fifteen-month-old with blonde curls and hazel eyes. We had no way of knowing, of course, that this baby would eventually become our daughter.

Although we heard no guarantee about our chances for adopting you, Daddy and I were encouraged after our meeting. Always superstitious, I began noticing encouraging signs everywhere. As silly as it sounds, even our fortune cookies seemed to bode well. The first cookie advised us to "Watch out for children." Another recommended patience: "Good things are coming to you in due course of time."

Of course, we were doing more than consuming Chinese takeout during this time. Our first assignment was finalizing our home study, which had already been initiated. In order to be approved as adoptive parents, Daddy and I underwent an extensive background check and attended several interview/counseling sessions with an independent social worker who questioned us carefully about our views on parenting. Several of our friends wrote letters of references, attesting to our ability to provide a safe and loving home.

Two months after hearing about you, we saw you for the first time in your foster home. Despite not feeling well, you gamely entertained us by dancing around the room with a plastic bucket on your head. You amazed everyone by playing with Daddy's beard and patiently allowing me to hold you in my lap and lace your shoes. We fell in love with you.

Daddy and I soon learned that we were officially qualified to be adoptive parents. However, there were numerous legal issues to be resolved before your placement could be approved. During this time, we visited with you periodically so you could become familiar with us. I even accompanied you to a doctor's appointment.

At the urging of the social worker, Daddy and I tackled

our next assignment—writing detailed autobiographies. This therapeutic exercise helped us temper our anxiety and impatience. As if to offer further encouragement, yet another fortune cookie promised us, "Good news is on the way."

In early spring, we did indeed receive some good news. Not only did your Uncle Mitch return safely to the United States following military duty in the Persian Gulf, but during an out-of-state trip to welcome him home, Daddy and I were tracked down by friends who relayed a long-anticipated message. Our social worker had called to say that one of the last legal hurdles delaying your placement had been cleared. Our prayers were being answered—we would soon be parents!

The excitement we felt during the next few weeks was at times mixed with apprehension. Although we were ecstatic about becoming parents, we worried that the change would be traumatic for you. We expected you to experience some feelings of loss after leaving the foster family you had known and loved for more than a year, and we wondered if we would be able to comfort you. Curiously, another prophetic fortune cookie allayed our anxieties with the comforting message, "You will win success in whatever you adopt."

May 16, 1991, was the happiest day of our lives. Early that morning before you arrived, I videotaped Daddy tying a bouquet of pink balloons on the mailbox. Afterwards, there was nothing to do except pace the floors in nervous anticipation until you, the social worker and your foster mother finally arrived at 11:00 A.M.

Our anxieties were instantly dispelled the moment you were placed in our arms. Smiling resolutely, you seemed to accept the ensuing commotion as normal. It seemed that the adults were the only ones stirred up.

Your foster mother thoughtfully provided detailed notes describing your medical history as well as your routine and favorite foods. This information, along with your collection of familiar toys, helped to make those first few days easier. Yes, there were some tears—especially when we placed you in that strange new crib. But you adjusted incredibly quickly to your new home and family.

In the four years since you became our daughter, you have grown in so many ways. Daddy and I are constantly amazed at your development, your personality and your sense of humor. We've accepted our fate as parents of a world-class punmeister. (How else to explain the puppet show you produced recently called "Goatilocks and the Three Bears"?)

Thank you, angel, for bringing us so much joy and love. Thank you for helping us become a family.

All my love,
Mommy

Civilization marches forward on the feet of healthy children.

—*Herbert Hoover*

Helping your eldest son pick a college is one of the great educational experiences in life—for the parents. Next to trying to pick his bride, it's the best way to learn that your authority, if not entirely gone, is slipping fast.

—*Sally and James Reston*

To show a child what has once delighted you, to find the child's delight added to your own, so that there is now a double delight seen in the glow of trust and affections, this is happiness.

—*J. B. Priestley*

It sometimes happens, even in the best of families, that a baby is born. This is not necessarily cause for alarm. The important thing is to keep your wits about you and borrow some money.

—*Elinor Goulding Smith*

I figure if the kids are alive at the end of the day, I've done my job.

— *Roseanne*

What good mothers and fathers instinctively feel like doing for their babies is usually best after all.

— *Dr. Benjamin Spock*

It is easier to have children than raise them.

— *Irish Saying*

Our children are here to stay, but our babies and toddlers and preschoolers are gone as fast as they can grow up — and we have only a short moment with each. When you see a grandfather take a baby in his arms, you see that the moment hasn't always been long enough.

— *Saint Clair Adams Sullivan*

Parenthood remains the greatest single preserve of the amateur.

—Alvin Toffler

A Sunday-school teacher was telling her five-year-olds about moral lessons in life. "Now, children, you must never do anything in private that you wouldn't do in public," she said. The sentence didn't go unnoticed, as one freckled-face sprite cheered: "Hooray! No more baths!"

—Eva Shaw

You don't choose your family. They are God's gift to you, as you are to them.

—Desmond Tutu

Reparative Narratives:
Helping Kids Heal in Hard Times
by Ava L. Siegler, Ph.D.

Parents have known for centuries that stories are an important way to teach children what they need to know. That is why every culture has its special stories, stories about little ones who outwit giants, or loyal children who save their parents' lives, or clever children who trick evil wizards, or greedy children who get their just rewards, or curious children who cause trouble. Stories are popular in all their forms in all cultures because human beings need narratives as ways of organizing, understanding and transforming their lives.

Narrative thought is a particularly important kind of thinking in childhood. It helps children to learn about the ways of the world, how to get along in the world, and how to get along with the people of the world. Sometimes a story will convey important information to your child; sometimes it may bridge a gap between your child's fantasy and a different reality; sometimes the story may help your child rehearse for an upcoming experience; and sometimes the story might help to repair a wound your child has suffered.

No matter how protective of our kids we try to be, we can't control their experiences, but we can have some control over the way our kids understand their experiences. Remember, words can heal as well as hurt. By using words to construct reparative narratives—narratives to help heal tough times—you can help your kids deal with many of the problems of today. These special stories can explain the ways of the world to your child as she grows, and they can interpret her experiences after she has them. What makes a narrative reparative is that it helps place a child's experience within that cushion of safety. By telling your kids stories about events—stories with a beginning, a middle and an end—we can help them find meaning in their lives and heal the unavoidable hurts.

For thousands of years, father and son have stretched wistful hands across the canyon of time, each eager to help the other to his side, but neither quite able to desert the loyalties of his contemporaries. The relationship is always changing and hence always fragile: Nothing endures except the sense of difference.

—Alan Valentine

It is not possible for civilization to flow backward while there is youth in the world. Youth may be headstrong, but it will advance its allotted length.

—Helen Keller

For parents of the Little Leaguer, a baseball game is simply a nervous breakdown into innings.

—Earl Wilson

On viewing the Pacific Ocean for the first time, a four-year-old Kansas native exclaimed: "Look, Daddy—it just keeps flushing and flushing!"

—Anonymous

Youth is, after all, just a moment, but it is the moment, the spark that you always carry in your heart.

—*Raisa M. Gorbachev*

I discovered when I had a child of my own that I had become a biased observer of small children. Instead of looking at them with affectionate but nonpartisan eyes, I saw each of them as older or younger, bigger or smaller, more or less graceful, intelligent or skilled than my own children.

—*Margaret Mead*

Some parents . . . say it is toy guns that make boys warlike. . . . But give a boy a rubber duck and he will seize its neck like the butt of a pistol and shout "Bang!"

—*George F. Will*

The Passionate Mind

by Michael Schulman

In observing and fostering your own child's creative development, try to avoid preconceptions about what a creative child is supposed to be like. Your child may develop a great passion for art and show early signs of creative potential, yet insist on dressing like a little banker.

Your child may develop a strong singular interest early and stay with it for the rest of his or her life, or may go through many changes and ultimately pursue more than one career. Whatever the external form, one of the great gifts of parenthood is having a close-up view of the blossoming of a creative and passionate mind.

Enjoy it.

I believe deeply that children are more powerful than oil, more beautiful than rivers, more precious than any other natural resource a country can have.

—*Danny Kaye*

There is no tragedy in life like the death of a child. Things never get back to the way they were.

—*Dwight D. Eisenhower*

You have a wonderful child. Then, when he's thirteen, gremlins carry him away and leave in his place a stranger who gives you not a moment's peace. . . . You have to hang in there, because two or three years later, the gremlins will return your child and he will be wonderful again.

—*Jill Eikenberry*

Life . . . would give her everything of consequence, life would shape her, not we. All we were good for was to make the introductions.

—*Helen Hayes*

A fundamental defect of fathers is that they want their children to be a credit to them.

— Bertrand Russell

The family is the place where the most ridiculous and least respectable things in the world go on.

— Ugo Betti

Even a secret agent can't lie to a Jewish mother.

— Peter Malkin

You don't raise heroes, you raise sons. And if you treat them like sons, they'll turn out to be heroes, even if it's just in your own eyes.

— Walter M. Schirra Sr.

I have found the best way to give advice to your children is to find out what they want and then advise them to do it.

— Harry S. Truman

A Good Enough Parent

by Bruno Bettelheim, Ph.D.

Many life experiences which would be commonplace to an adult are overwhelming to a child. Adults have learned to know, accept and even anticipate them. None of this is true for children; for them, many experiences are entirely new and unexpected. Even events that have become well known to a somewhat older child are exciting or overwhelming to the young child because of his inexperience.

Only rarely does a grown-up encounter the unusual, the very exciting, the threatening and unexpected occurrence. But such events are the rule rather than the exception for the young child, even though the occurrence itself may seem ordinary, innocuous, or even pleasant to the adult observer.

It's clear that most American children suffer too much mother and too little father.

—*Gloria Steinem*

From the moment the baby first turns his eyes to the light, or shows that she has noticed a sound; from the time he first reaches out for his rattle or for the finger held invitingly near or toward the smiling face above her; from the moment he kicks and coos with delight as someone who loves him comes near; from the moment she responds with evident joy to some light, some color, some sound; in short, from tiniest babyhood on, a child is reaching out with eagerness to take the world by a tiny grasp. He reaches out to feel, to taste, to touch, to hold. She reaches out for color and light and sound. He searches for meanings.

Even before the baby can talk one hears the questioning in her tones and sees it in her actions. When words begin to come he questions why, why of anyone who will answer him. She revels in new understandings as they unfold to her searching thought. He shows his delight in beauty as it is revealed to him in word, in rhythm, in sound, in color, in the color, in the love of the people around him. She glories in her ability to do, in her accomplishment, in her achievements. He has his ups and downs, his babyhood problems, the trials of childhood, but they are all a part of understanding the mysteries of living, of finding his place in the universe and his relationships to the beings who people his world. Daily new meanings unfold for this child in thought, new understandings are imparted on her, new abilities are revealed—and with what joy she accepts them all!

—*Grace Langdon, Ph.D.*

Five Ways

by *Marcos Behean Hernandez*

Parents can do much toward actively helping their children develop and mature into responsible adults. There are five major concepts that parents can apply to do this.

First, and most important, they can begin to openly and honestly communicate with their children.

Second, they can take an active interest in their children's school life and work closely with teachers and other parents.

Third, they can help to foster desirable values and attitudes in their children, particularly those values and attitudes relating to productive social behavior.

Fourth, they can provide constant encouragement and love to their children, especially during times of difficulty.

Finally, parents can, by a variety of means, help their children develop positive self-images and strong character traits.

When you read about a car crash in which two or three youngsters are killed, do you pause to dwell on the amount of love and treasure and patience parents poured into bodies no longer suitable for open caskets?

—Jim Bishop

Love your children with all your heart, love them enough to discipline them before it is too late. . . . Praise them for important things, even if you have to stretch them a bit. Praise them a lot. They live on it like bread and butter and they need it more than bread and butter.

—Lavina Christensen Fugal

Never promise something to a child and not give it to him, because in that way he learns to lie.

—The Talmud

I Remember Grandma

by Lois Wyse

A child who has a grandparent has a softened view of life, the feeling that there is more to life than what we see, more than getting and gaining, winning and losing.

There is a love that makes no demands.

We share so much with our grandchildren. For both grandparent and grandchild, the parents are the sometime enemy—both of us have protested the actions of those parents without giving up our love for them. Yet we share the knowledge with our grandchildren that we would not have one another if it were not for those parents.

Most of us are not the rule makers with our grandchildren; we have the fun of being rule breakers with them.

We get the joys of parenting without the midnight sniffles and the daytime coughs, without the need for discipline and the demand for obedience.

We are the recess, the play period, the respite from the demands made as they learn to live in a confusing world—and so our grandchildren look to us for good times and laughter.

Is it any wonder that we think grandchildren are so much fun?

Our children are not going to be just "our children"—
they are going to be other people's husbands and wives and
the parents of our grandchildren.

—*Mary S. Calderone*

Childhood is frequently a solemn business for those
inside it.

—*George F. Will*

One way to keep youth from slipping away is to hide the
car keys.

—*F. Robert Becker*

No matter how many communes anybody invents, the
family always creeps back.

—*Margaret Mead*

The father is always a Republican toward his son and his
mother's always a Democrat.

—*Robert Frost*

A Bit of Newspaper Verse
from the National Magazine Contest (1906)

She took up one of the magazines and glanced through it casually, but somehow it did not appeal to the old lady, and so she laid it down again. There was a volume of poems, richly bound in vellum, on the table by her side and for a while the story of its gallant knights and lovely maidens bewitched her. But soon the weight of the book began to tire her feeble hands.

After that, quite as a last resort, she took up the evening paper and glanced through it, just to wile away the time. She had never taken much concern in politics, the latest Parisian fashion did not interest her in the least, but presently three little verses, wedged in between a lurid account of a murder and a patent medicine advertisement, caught the eye.

The poem was Eugene Field's "Little Boy Blue," and at the very first lines of it the old lady became all attention:

> The little toy dog is covered with dust,
> But sturdy and staunch it stands,
> And the little tin soldier is covered with rust,
> And his musket molds in his hands.

Very slowly as she read on, the tears came into her eyes and dimmed the spectacles so that she could scarcely see the lines of the second verse:

"Now don't you go til I come," he said,
"And don't you make any noise!"
Then, toddling off to his trundle bed,
He dreamed of his pretty toys.
And as he was dreaming, an angel song
Awakened our little boy.
Oh, the years are many . . .

Yes, they are many! It was more than half a century ago now. The paper dropped from the old lady's hand and rustled to the floor. There was no use in trying to read anymore, for her thoughts had flown away now to the time when she had just such a Little Boy Blue as that. Since then she had lots of other children.

Even now, as the woman sat there in the twilight, she could hear the shouts of her grandchildren at play not far away, but little Geordie had been her firstborn and somehow the others were different, and nobody knew just how but herself. She had daughters to console her in her widowhood, and when her married daughter had died her children had been left to their grandmother for care.

But with little Geordie it was different. They only knew of him by the little headstone in the graveyard: but to her — why, after reading that little poem, it seemed as though it were only yesterday that he was toddling along beside her, rosy and bright and full of fun. And he used to say just those things . . . she remembered.

"Why, Mother," said her daughter, as she came in, "you've been crying! What's the matter?"

"It's nothing, dear," answered the older woman, as she wiped her eyes. "I was reading, you know, and it upset me a little . . . it was only a bit of newspaper verse."

Child-rearing is fascinating, exhausting, exciting, frustrating—and deeply rewarding. It is full of comedy, drama, sheer poetry—and sometimes tragedy, and you can never know in advance how it is going to be.

—*Sheila Kitzinger and Celia Kitzinger*

My mother groan'd
my father wept,
Into the dangerous world
I leapt.

—*William Blake*

When a child takes "no" for an answer, the kid is thinking of another way of asking the question.

—*Eva Shaw*

That innocence, that honesty, that logic—they are childhood. They are the Fountain of Youth for which Ponce de Leon was searching.

—*Bill Cosby*

It is a wise child that knows its own father.

—Iroquois Proverb

Before I got married, I had six theories about bringing up children. Now I have six children, and no theories.

—Lord Rochester

Boy, patting a cat and then placing his ear to that furry body: "He must be talking to somebody—I can hear the busy signal."

—Anonymous

When children are treated as if you really believe that they are intelligent beings, they will often show surprisingly good sense. It's easy to behave irresponsibly when someone else makes all the decisions for you.

—Michael Schulman and Eva Mekler

To bring up a child in the way he should go, travel that way yourself once in a while.

—Josh Billings

Inspiration and Perspiration
by Dorothy Rich, Ph.D.

The long list of school "problems" includes men and women who grew up to be distinguished adults. Among them are the authors Thomas Mann, Pearl Buck and Willa Cather; the inventor Henry Ford; the dancer Isadora Duncan; the scientist Albert Einstein; the composer Edvard Grieg. Disastrous school experiences of creative people are almost commonplace.

At the same time that author William Saroyan was a terrible school problem, he read every book in the Fresno, California, public library. Sigrid Undset, another well-known author, couldn't stand the school's freedom-curbing discipline. . . . Among school dropouts are the Wright Brothers, Thomas Edison, Pablo Picasso, Dimitri Shostakovich, Marchese Guglielmo Marconi, Noel Coward, Mark Twain and Pablo Casals.

Those who stayed in school had similar difficulties. Einstein, who was slow of speech, wanted to learn in his own way. He believed examinations, with their insistence on memorized facts, impeded education, which he felt was based on a "perpetual sense of wonder." It is said that he had a terrible time passing the usual school examinations, as did the composer Giacomo Puccini and the scientist Paul Ehrlich.

Writers who couldn't make the grade in class but who took literary honors afterward include Proust (his teachers said his compositions were disorganized), Stephen Crane, Eugene O'Neill, William Faulkner and F. Scott Fitzgerald.

Giftedness is a mixture of heredity and environment, and it's not absolutely clear how much of each ingredient goes into the recipe. You can do everything "right" and still not have a gifted child. You can do a lot wrong and have a gifted child.

One of the things I've discovered in general about raising kids is that they really don't give a damn if you walked five miles to school.

—*Patty Duke*

Parenting is an ongoing challenge.

—*Cynthia Whitham, M.S.W.*

For children . . . are, of all our possessions, infinitely the most valuable. They are our future; they are our purity; they are those who ask the vital questions we used to ask at their age, before we became intoxicated by the maelstrom of answers, the heady delights of personal opinion, the joys and sorrows of maturity.

—*Peter Ustinov*

We are the world; these are our children.

—*Harry Belafonte*

In helping children to find a spiritual dimension to life, it may be better to draw on and to trust their own deeply felt experiences than to superimpose our adult ideas.

The secondhand religion we offer is unlikely to hold deep meaning for them. What we teach them may later be rejected. But their own experiences will always have validity.

—Sheila Kitzinger and Celia Kitzinger

Little boy crying to a sales clerk in a large department store: "Have you seen a lady without a kid that looks just like me?"

—Eva Shaw

To watch our children making mistakes that could have been prevented is heartbreaking, for when they suffer, we suffer, too. Serious problems can and do occur in the very best of families, and sometimes they cannot be anticipated or avoided.

—Joan Wester Anderson

Accepting the fact of physical or developmental disability can be particularly challenging both for the child who has special health needs and for the nondisabled child. Meeting the problem head-on often decreases the discomfort on both sides. Parents of disabled children and parents of nondisabled kids need to help their children discover that a disabled person is still a person in every way.

—Karyn Feiden

In dealing with children
the left hand should push them away and
the right hand should draw them near.

—Rabbi Shimon ben Elazar

Some parents have trouble selecting a name for their new baby—others have wealthy relatives.

—Anonymous

I believe the power of observation in numbers of very young children to be quite wonderful for its closeness and accuracy. Indeed, I think that most grown men who are remarkable in this respect, may with greater propriety be said not to have lost the faculty, than to have acquired it; rather, as generally observed such men retain a certain freshness, and gentleness, and capacity of being pleased, which are also an inheritance they have preserved from their childhood.

—Charles Dickens

When Charles first saw our child Mary, he said all the proper things for a new father. He looked upon the poor little red thing and blurted, "She's more beautiful than the Brooklyn Bridge."

—Helen Hayes

Noble Boys

by Clarence Day

Like most children [of the 1890s], I was taught to admire high ideals in my boyhood. Those teachings were well-meant of course, and I took them all in good part. I really didn't admire some of the ideals much, and I made no attempt to live up to them, but at least regarded such things with a wary respect. Though they sounded to me like standards meant for much better boys than myself, I saw that I too would have to adopt them if I ever became really good, and consequently it interested me to hear about them and filled me with awe—much the same kind of awe I felt at ghost stories, only more far-off and solemn. Meantime they brought home to me the acute disadvantage of goodness, and kept me content with not having very great moral ambitions.

These doses of high ideals came in various ways, each one unexpected. Sometimes they were administered to me in the form of little talks by my teachers. Sometimes they appeared in a book. On my seventh birthday, for instance, old Mrs. Caister gave me *The Christmas Child* by Mrs. Molesworth. This child's name was Ted, and his history was given at great length from his babyhood to the day he was twelve. I read it all the way through, because a book is a book, but although this one had bright red covers and pictures, it was kind of depressing.

It began with a lot of Ted's cunning baby talk. I had to

skip some of that. I went on as fast as I could till Ted was seven, like me. But at this point I ran into a long account of his unselfish acts . . . and according to Mrs. Molesworth, he was "a boy of nice feelings. Not rough and knockabout in his ways like many schoolboys," she added, in what I felt was a reproving tone directed to me. . . . It was plain that Ted had all the virtues.

Ted died at the end of the book, just before his twelfth birthday. Very good children often did die on the last page, I had noticed. They never had anything violent or awful the matter with them, they just took sick and expired very gently of some vague and unnamed diseases.

I didn't like books with unhappy endings, but I didn't mind this one. It seemed sad, in a way, and yet suitable. I regarded it with much the same feelings that I later regarded Greek tragedies. The Olympian deities in their hate stacked the cards against Oedipus and Jehovah, and Mrs. Molesworth did the same thing to Ted, out of love. It was a comfort to feel that heaven neither loved nor hated me yet, and I earnestly hoped that it never would. I felt pretty sure that I could get along all right by myself, if heaven would ignore my existence and let me alone.

Those who speak of it as being easy to take candy away from a baby should try it sometime.

—Anonymous

Wherever children are learning, there dwells the Divine Presence.

—Hebrew Proverb

During the teen years, our children enter a new and exciting phase of their lives. If an adolescent is experiencing difficulty with this development change, it may be that we parents are still holding on too tight to their concerns.

By letting go we help not only ourselves, but also our teens by showing them how to become more responsible. No one grows up if someone else is taking care of all their problems.

—Betty Fish and Raymond Fish

I didn't belong as a kid, and that always bothered me. If only I'd known that one day my differentness would be an asset, then my early life would have been much easier.

—Bette Midler

Listen when you're talking!
Don't say you're right all the time, teacher!
Let the pupils discover it!
Don't force the truth too far:
It won't stand it.
Listen when you're talking!

—*Bertolt Brecht*

A child whose mother works in a soup kitchen once a week is more likely to volunteer to help others. A child who sees his father do favors ungrudgingly for his friends is more likely to be generous himself. Parents can also talk to their child about what they are doing and why, including the pleasure it gives them to help others.

—*The Children's Television Network*

"You're getting more handsome than your dad," a proud mom told her little boy.

"Of course," replied the child, "I'm a later model!"

—*Eva Shaw*

Joy! Joy expressed at home and being brought up in a largely joyous, smiling, laughing household is a blessing indeed. It provides the lesson to the child. It gives endless, wonderful memories. It is the gut stuff of self-esteem because in being joyous we tap all of our inner resources, integrate them, and feel them in this most human way of all.

—*Theodore Isaac Rubin, M.D.*

Setting a good example for your children takes all the fun out of middle age.

—*William Feather*

If children are old enough to talk, they are old enough to begin to understand and appreciate their parents saying: "I'm sorry. I made a mistake." Children see their parents as more human, more compassionate, and respect them more for apologizing. It's unfair for a parent to insist that a child apologize when that parent never admits to a mistake.

—*Lee Salk, M.D.*

Summer Children

by Edgar A. Guest

I like 'em in the winter when their cheeks are slightly pale,
I like 'em in the spring time when the March winds blow a
    gale;
But when summer suns have tanned 'em and they're racing
    to and fro,
I somehow think the children make the finest sort of show.

When they're brown as little berries and they're bare of foot
    and head,
And they're on the go each minute where the velvet lawns
    are spread,
Then their health is at its finest and they never stop to rest,
Oh, it's then I think the children look and are their very best.

We've got to know the winter and we've got to know the
    spring,
But for children, could I do it, unto summer I would cling;
For I'm happiest when I see 'em, as a wild and merry band
Of healthy, lusty youngsters that the summer sun has tanned.

A youngster devoted a sleeting and dismally gray afternoon to drawing with a brand new of set of crayons. Mother looked over the tot's shoulder and finally gave in to curiosity. "Who's that you're drawing, honey?"

"God," came the answer.

"Don't be silly, love. Nobody knows what God looks like."

Not even pausing in the task, the child announced calmly, "They will when I'm finished!"

—*Eva Shaw*

If newborns could remember and speak, they would emerge from the womb carrying tales as wondrous as Homer's.

—*Newsweek*

For parents today, it is tempting to see abductors around every corner, nitrates in every hot dog, roundworms in every sandbox. But children see the world filled with fascinating things: new people, greasy hot dogs and inviting sandboxes. And often, in spite of the doom-and-gloom headlines, they are right.

Children also tend to accept the world for what it is, for that is all they know. The problems and dangers they and their friends might face are familiar, if unpleasant, aspects of their landscape. When parents talk of a changing world, then, it is a world that has changed for them, not for their children.

—*The Children's Television Network*

Babies: a loud noise at the one end and no sense of responsibility at the other.

—Monsignor Ronald Knox

A sanctuary is a refuge, a safe house in which the spirit as well as the body can be protected from harm. It is your job, as a protective parent, to create this sanctuary for your children, even if you yourself have doubts about the future of our earth, even if you yourself are filled with dread at each new scientific discovery that reveals how our world has been contaminated.

Even if you yourself have no faith at all in the possibility of rescue or repair of the damage we've done to ourselves, your children deserve to be protected from your darkest thoughts.

—Ava L. Siegler, Ph.D.

A father is a thing that growls when it feels good—and laughs loud when scared half to death.

—Paul Harvey

There is a sense of accomplishment that comes with the mission of passing on life to another tiny human being, who will embody not only your own qualities, but those of your ancestors as well.

—Grace Langdon, Ph.D.

We parents are the holders of a priceless gift, a gift we received from countless generations we never knew, a gift that we only now possess and only we can give our children. That unique gift, of course, is the gift of ourselves. Whatever we can do to give that gift, and to help others receive it, is worth the challenge of all our human endeavor.

—Mister (Fred) Rogers

Character builds slowly, but it can be torn down with incredible swiftness.

—Faith Baldwin

Young and old come forth to play
On a sunshine holiday.

—John Milton

Children need models more than they need critics.

—Joseph Joubert

Little Women Plan Christmas

by Louisa May Alcott

"Christmas won't be Christmas without any presents," grumbled Jo, lying on the rug.

"It's so dreadful to be poor," sighed Meg, looking down at her old dress.

"I don't think it's fair for some girls to have plenty of pretty things, and other girls nothing at all," added little Amy, with an injured sniff.

"We've got Father and Mother and each other," said Beth contentedly, from her corner.

The four young faces on which the firelight shone brightened at the cheerful words, but darkened again as Jo said sadly, "We haven't got Father, and shall not have him for a long time." She didn't say "perhaps never," but each silently added it, thinking of Father far away, where the fighting was.

Nobody spoke for a minute; then Meg said in an altered tone, "You know the reason Mother proposed not having any presents this Christmas because it is going to be a hard winter for everyone; and she thinks we ought not to spend money for pleasure, when our men are suffering so in the army. We can't do much, but we can make our little sacrifices, and ought to do it gladly. But I am afraid I don't." And Meg shook her head, as she thought regretfully of all the pretty things she wanted.

"But I don't think the little we should spend would do any good. We've each got a dollar, and the army wouldn't be mush helped by our giving that. I agree not to expect anything from Mother or you, but I do want to buy Undine and Sintram for myself; I've wanted it so long," said Jo, who was a bookworm.

"I planned to spend mine on new music," said Beth, with a little sigh, which no one heard but the hearth brush and kettle holder.

"I shall get a nice box of drawing pencils; I really need them," said Amy decidedly.

"Mother didn't say anything about our money, and she won't wish us to give up everything. Let's each buy what we want, and have a little fun; I'm sure we work hard enough to earn it," cried Jo, examining the heels of her shoes in a gentlemanly manner.

The clock struck six; and, having swept up the hearth, Beth put a pair of slippers down to warm. Somehow the sight of the old shoes had a good effect upon the girls, for Mother was coming, and everyone brightened to welcome her. Meg stopped lecturing, and lighted the lamp, Amy got out of the easy chair without being asked, and Jo forgot how tired she was as she sat up to hold the slippers nearer to the blaze.

"They are quite worn out; Marmee must have a new pair."

"I thought I'd get her some with my dollar," said Beth.

"No, I shall!" cried Amy.

"I'm the oldest," began Meg.

But Jo cut in with a decided, "I'm the man in the family now that Papa is away, and I shall provide the slippers, for he told me to take special care of Mother while he was gone."

"I'll tell you what we'll do," said Beth. "Let's each get her something for Christmas, and not get anything for ourselves."

"That's like you, dear! What will we get?" exclaimed Jo.

Everyone thought soberly for a minute. Then Meg announced, as if the idea was suggested by the sight of her own pretty hands, "I shall give her a nice pair of gloves."

"Army shoes, best to be had," cried Jo.

"Some handkerchiefs, all hemmed," said Beth.

"I'll get a bottle of cologne," said Amy.

"How will we give the things?" asked Meg.

"Put them on the table and bring her in and see her open the bundles," answered Jo. "Don't you remember how we used to do it on our birthdays?"

Many parents worry that they are . . . bribing and that this is harmful for this child. First of all, children may think they are doing the chore/behavior for the token, sticker, or treat. But actually, they are doing it for the social reinforcer, the praise that you give when you give the token.

— *Cynthia Whitham, M.S.W.*

It's one of the mysteries of life why fathers should worry so about their sons . . . they used to be one themselves.

— *Eva Shaw*

I firmly believe that trying to educate children without the involvement of the families is like trying to play a basketball game without all the players on the court.

— *Senator Bill Bradley*

Our children will one day be conducting the business of our society. If we bring them up to recognize the benefits of cooperation rather than competition and to consider the impact of their business activities on others, then perhaps a new economic system in which morality has a larger place will evolve.

— *Michael Schulman and Eva Mekler*

Proud mother, holding infant for coworkers to see: "He's beginning to eat solids now — keys, books, pencils . . . "

—*Eva Shaw*

When parents and children do something constructive together, a special something happens. If there are tensions, especially as children grow older, they seem to evaporate, or at least they don't get in the way. There's a feeling of cooperation, almost like a runner's high. It may not be chemical, but it's real.

—*Dorothy Rich, Ph.D.*

It is not a bad thing that children should occasionally, and politely, put parents in their place.

—*Colette*

What a parent should save for a rainy day is patience.

—*Anonymous*

Raising children is like making biscuits: It is as easy to raise a big batch as one, while you have your hands in the dough.

—*E. W. Howe*

Everyone loves the old fairy tale ending: "And so they were married and lived happily ever after." But in my opinion the best part of any true-life story only begins with these words.

Certainly life's greatest challenge is raising a family. My own life has been exciting, rich and immensely rewarding in every way. I have been lucky enough to win fame and fortune beyond my dreams. And yet, the greatest and most satisfying success by far that I have enjoyed lies in my children. Helping them, watching them grow, has been my greatest joy and privilege.

My five "Links" represent what I'd like America to remember about me.

—*Art Linkletter*

A characteristic of the normal child is he doesn't act that way very often.

—*Franklin P. Jones*

Your children need your presence more than your presents.

—*Reverend Jesse Jackson*

Every baby born into the world is a finer one than the last.

—*Charles Dickens*

Many a parent's life is disorganized around children.

—*Anonymous*

There are only two lasting bequests we can hope to give our children. One of these is roots, the other wings.

—*Hodding Carter*

In daily living, tears and fights and doing things we don't want to do are all part of our human ways of developing into adults.

—*Mister (Fred) Rogers*

To teenagers: Straighten up your room first, then the world.

—*Jeff Jordon*

If you always do what interests you, then at least one person is pleased.

—*Advice to Katharine Hepburn from her mother*

Was there ever a grandparent, bushed after a day of minding those precious little bundles of trouble, who hasn't bet the good Lord knew what he was doing when he gave little children to young people?

—*Eva Shaw*

Never have children, only grandchildren.

—*Gore Vidal*

A Child's Legacy

by Cecil Rhodes

No one should leave money to his children. It is a curse to them. What we should do for our children, if we do them the best service we can, is to give them the best education we can procure for them, and then turn them loose in the world without a sixpence for themselves.

What happens when you leave them a fortune? They no longer have a spur to effort.

Where there is shouting, there is not true knowledge.

—Leonardo da Vinci

By giving children lots of affection, you can help fill them with love and acceptance of themselves. Then that's what they will have to give away.

—Dr. Wayne Dyer

To love and be loved is to feel the sun from both sides.

—David Viscott

A child miseducated is a child lost.

—John F. Kennedy

When I was a kid my parents moved a lot—but I always found them.

—Rodney Dangerfield

We are given children to test us and make us more spiritual.

—*George F. Will*

See how happy children are, smiling and laughing, radiating so much energy and bliss. With all our wisdom and understanding, we rarely exude such bliss.

—*Swami Shantanand Saraswati*

Seven-year-old Emily was invited to visit her great-aunt in Boston. Along with all the last-minute instructions, her mom added: "Remember that Aunt Maude is persnickety: If you have to go to the bathroom, be sure to say, 'Excuse me, I'd like to powder my nose.'"

Emily made an incredible hit with her great-aunt and the two became close, joyful friends regardless of the seventy-year age difference. When Emily was getting ready to return home, the aunt said, "I loved having you here, darling. On your next visit, perhaps your little sister Jennifer will be able to come with you."

"I'd better not bring her, Auntie," Emily said quickly. "Jennifer still powders her nose in bed."

—*Bennet Cerf*

To a newborn . . .
Sometimes I marvel at how sweet you are;
Sometimes I marvel at how strong you are;
Sometimes I just marvel.

—Eva Shaw

Children make the most desirable opponents in Scrabble as they are both easy to beat and fun to cheat.

—Fran Lebowitz

Keep in mind that the true meaning of an individual is how he treats a person who can do him absolutely no good.

—Ann Landers

Having a family is like having a bowling alley installed in your brain.

—Martin Mull

Families with babies and families without babies are sorry for each other.

—E. W. Howe

Faults are thick where love is thin.

—*James Howell*

A man can't get rich if he takes proper care of his family.

—*Navajo Saying*

Whatever you do to your child's body, you are doing to your child's mind, too.

—*Penelope Leach*

Let your children go if you want to keep them.

—*Malcolm Forbes*

Gangs are a group reaction to helplessness.

—*Reverend Jesse Jackson*

Children can learn to cope with many scary things in life—violence on television included—so long as they have caring adults at hand who want to help them. Watching television with our children, and talking about it, is the best way to keep violence on television from becoming overwhelming and damaging.

—Mister (Fred) Rogers

Don't make a baby if you can't be a father.

—National Urban League Slogan

The most important thing a father can do for his children is love their mother.

—Theodore Hesburgh

The young always have the same problem—how to rebel and conform at the same time. They have solved this by defying their parents and copying one another.

—Quentin Crisp

Without a family, man, alone in the world, trembles with the cold.

—*André Maurois*

Every mother is like Moses. She does not enter the promised land. She prepares a world she will not see.

—*Pope Paul VI*

Never fret for an only son, the idea of failure will never occur to him.

—*George Bernard Shaw*

Never allow your child to call you by your first name. He hasn't known you long enough.

—*Fran Lebowitz*

Parents are like cars—built-in obsolescence.

—*Harvey Lacy*, Cagney & Lacy

What Is a Girl?

by Alan Beck

A little girl can be sweeter (and badder) oftener than anyone else in the world. She can jitter around, and stomp, and make funny noises that frazzle your nerves, yet just when you open your mouth she stands there demure with that special look in her eyes.

A girl is Innocence playing in the mud, Beauty standing on its head, and Motherhood dragging a doll by the foot.

What Is a Boy?

by Alan Beck

Boys are found everywhere—on top of, underneath, inside of, climbing on, swinging from, running around or jumping to. Mothers love them, little girls hate them, older sisters and brothers tolerate them, adults ignore them and heaven protects them.

A boy is Truth with dirt on its face, Beauty with a cut on its finger, Wisdom with bubble gum in its hair, and Hope of the future with a frog in its pocket.

Heredity is what sets the parents of a teenager wondering about each other.

—*Laurence J. Peter*

All children alarm their parents, if only because you are forever expecting to encounter yourself.

—*Gore Vidal*

Love doesn't just sit there, like a stone; it has to be made, like bread, remade all the time, made new.

—*Ursula K. LeGuin*

A lady of forty-seven who has been married twenty-seven years and has six children knows what love really is and once described it for me like this: "Love is what you've been through with somebody."

—*James Thurber*

The real lost souls don't wear their hair long and play guitars. They have crew cuts, trained minds, sign on for research in biological warfare and don't give their parents a moment's worry.

—*J. B. Priestley*

Individuality: the quality that makes any two children different—especially if one is yours and the other isn't.

—*Eva Shaw*

The traits that a disobedient child gets are from the other parent.

—*Luther Burbank*

Children are born motivated, not bored. They come out into the world eager, reaching, looking, touching—and that's what we want them to keep on doing.

—*Dorothy Rich, Ph.D.*

If your parents didn't have children, there is a good chance that you won't have any.

—*Clarence Day*

Twelve Rules That Don't Change

Anonymous

1. Don't disapprove of what a child is—disapprove of the actions.
2. Give attention and praise for good behavior, not for bad behavior.
3. Parents should allow and encourage discussion, but the parent makes the final decision.
4. Punishment should be reasonable and related to the offense.
5. Throw out all rules that you are unwilling to enforce, and be willing to change rules if you think it reasonable to do so.
6. Don't lecture and don't warn. Youngsters can remember things they think are important to remember.
7. Don't feel you have to justify rules, although you should be willing to explain them.
8. As your youngsters get old, many rules may be flexible and subject to discussion and compromise. However, on those few rules you really feel strongly about, enforce them even if other parents have a different rule.
9. Allow the child or youth to assume responsibility for decisions as he or she shows the ability to do so.
10. Don't expect children to show more self-control than you do as a parent.

11. Be honest with your youngster—hypocrisy shows.
12. The most important thing in your youngster's self-image is what he or she thinks you think. Self-image is a major factor in how the youngster thinks and what he or she does.

Education is helping a child realize his potentialities.

—*Erich Fromm*

If you don't respect your parents, your child will not respect you.

—*Maimonides*

Adults often tell children, "Grow up." Perhaps one of the wisest things adults can do is to "grow down"—to do or say something from time to time, as children frequently do, that makes little or no sense.

—*Allen Klein*

All happy families are alike, but every unhappy one is unhappy in its own way.

—*Leo Tolstoy*

Encourage your child to use his or her creativity. Often, the simplest idea can blossom into an hour's entertainment. All that is needed is a supportive adult (with a sense of humor), a suggestion or two, and a child's imagination.

—*Leslie Hamilton*

If you think education is expensive, try failure.

—*John Condry*

A small boy invaded the lingerie section of a major department store and shyly presented his problem to the sales clerk. "I want to buy my mom a present of a slip for her birthday," he said, "but I'm darned if I know what size she wears."

The clerk said, "It would help to know if your mom is tall or short, or skinny or large."

"Why—she's just perfect," beamed the youngster, so the clerk wrapped up a size-8 slip and the boy dashed down the aisle to meet a gray-haired couple, obviously the boy's grandparents.

Two days later, a woman came into the store and as chance had it, told the same clerk about her eight-year-old's present. The slip? She exchanged the size 8 for a size 22 short.

—*Anonymous*

A father never knew it could be so difficult to raise a child. A grandfather never knew it could be so easy.

—*Eva Shaw*

Discipline is the last thing that a father wants to consider because he doesn't like taking on tasks for which he has no talent. His only comfort is that no one else has any talent either: It is a game with seeded players. In fact, the great unspoken truth about child-raising is that, in spite of the 7,000 books of expert advice, the right way to discipline a child is still a mystery to most fathers, and to most mothers, too. Only your grandmother and Genghis Khan knew how to do it.

—Bill Cosby

The teacher who can arouse a feeling for one single good action, for one single good poem, accomplishes more than he who fills our memory with rows and rows of natural objects, classified with name and form.

—Goethe

My Twelve Loveliest Things, People Not Counted

(an interview with a Scottish child, c. 1850)
by Dr. Douglas Horton

The scrunch of dry leaves as you walk through them
The feel of clean clothes
Water running into the bath
The cold of ice cream
Cool wind on a hot day
Climbing up and looking back
Honey in your mouth
Smell of a drugstore
Hot-water bottle in bed
Babies smiling
The feeling inside when you sing
Baby animals

A sign of growing up: Little girls who used to make faces at boys are now making eyes at them.

—*Anonymous*

Many parents get great enjoyment with a child as he or she goes exploring, experimenting, questioning, investigating, enjoying through the days. The child, too, gets such a thrill of enjoyment out of each new thing discovered, out of each new bit of understanding that comes, out of every new-found ability, out of every bit of doing and accomplishment, out of the difficulties, that the parent with a seeing eye and an understanding heart can get real pleasure in sharing that enjoyment.

It is very important for a child to have his parents enjoy him, enjoy the things he does, enjoy things with him—it is the beginning of a companionship that can make living rich for both parents and child. It can begin in early babyhood and all through the years. And how it can grow with a little nourishing and cherishing!

—*Grace Langdon, Ph.D.*

A suburban mother's role is to deliver children obstetrically once, and by car forever after.

—*Peter de Vries*

A family is a unit composed not only of children but of men, women, an occasional animal and the common cold.

—*Ogden Nash*

The child is quiet, and his curls
Are full of evening light,
He sits in utter confidence
On the edge of night.

—*Robert P. Tristram Coffin*

The Timeless House of Children's Games

from Sports Illustrated

Any parent who has ever found a rusted toy automobile buried in the grass or a bent sand bucket on the beach knows that objects like these can be among the most powerful things in the world. They can summon up an instant, in colors stronger than life, the whole of childhood at its happiest—the disproportionate affection lavished on some strange possession, the concentrated self-forgetfulness of play, the elusive expressions of surprise or elation that pass so transparently over youthful features.

A child of one can be taught not to do certain things such as touch a hot stove, turn on the gas, pull lamps off their tables by their cords, or wake Mommy before noon.

—Joan Rivers

A small girl watched a passing boy and girl and turned to her friend. "Why, she's old enough to be his sitter!"

—Anonymous

Mother is the name for God in the lips and hearts of little children.

— William Makepeace Thackeray

Children think not of what is past, nor what is to come, but enjoy the present time, which few of us do.

—Jean de La Bruyere

Children are a bridge to heaven.

—Persian Proverb

Did you hear about the young upscale couple who always refer to their nursery as the "bawlroom"?

—Eva Shaw

There is more happiness in a multitude of children than safety in a multitude of counselors; and if I were a rich man, I should like to have twenty children.

—Sydney Smith

Your children are not your children.

—Kahlil Gibran

I was ever of opinion that the honest man who married and brought up a large family did more service than he who continued single and only talked of population.

—Oliver Goldsmith

Children are hopes.

—Novalis

His Father Is Satisfied

from the Chicago Advance, *c. 1885*

A very young, discouraged doctor, just graduated from medical school and practicing in our large city, was visited by his father, who came up from a rural district to look after his boy.

"Well, son," he said, "how are you getting along?"

"I'm not getting along at all," was the disheartened answer. "I'm not doing a thing."

The older man's countenance fell, but he spoke of courage and patience and perseverance. Later in the day he went with his son to the Free Dispensary, where the young doctor had an unsalaried position, and where he spent an hour or more every day.

The father sat by, a silent but intensely interested spectator, while twenty-five poor unfortunates received help. The doctor forgot his visitor while he bent his skilled energies to his task; but hardly had the doctor closed on the last patient when the older man burst forth:

"I thought you told me that you were not doing anything! Why, if I had helped twenty-five people in a month as much as you have in one morning, I would thank God that my life counted for something."

"There isn't any money in it, though," explained the son, somewhat abashed.

"Money!" the older man shouted, still scornfully. "Money!

What is money in comparison with being of use to your fellow human beings! Never mind about money; you go right along at this work every day. I'll go back to the farm and gladly earn money enough to support you as long as I live—yes, and sleep soundly every night with the thought that I have helped you to help humanity."

Five-year-old: noise with dirt on it.

—*Anonymous*

Children's children are the crown of old men;
And fathers are the pride of their children.

—*Prv. 17:6*

Families, like individuals, are unique. Cherish your family connections. They are one of God's greatest ways of demonstrating his love and fellowship.

—*Norman Vincent Peale*

When I was a boy of fourteen, my father was so ignorant I could hardly stand to have the old man around. But when I got to be twenty-one, I was astonished at how much he had learned in seven years.

—*Mark Twain*

You're never too old to do goofy stuff.

—*Ward Cleaver*
Leave It to Beaver

Speaking personally, I have found the happiness of parenthood greater than any other that I have experienced.

—Bertrand Russell

He who raises a child is to be called its father, not the man who only gave it birth.

—Midrash

A pre-teen was pawing over the cards in a stationery store when the clerk asked: "Just what is it you're looking for? Birthday card? Anniversary card for Mom and Dad? Get-well card for a teacher?"

With a sigh, the request came: "Got anything in the way of blank report cards?"

—Anonymous

A lot of parents pack up their troubles and send them off to summer camp.

—Raymond Duncan

There are no illegitimate children—only illegitimate parents.

—Judge Leon R. Yankwich

The only time a woman wishes she were a year older is when she is expecting a baby.

—Mary Marsh

A mother understands what a child does not say.

—Jewish Saying

Earthly paradise: the parents young, the children small.

—Victor Hugo

Creative minds always have been known to survive any kind of bad training.

—Anna Freud

No Recipe for Creativity

by Kenneth R. Blessing, Ph.D.

Children who produce many original ideas or have unique talents are labeled gifted or academically talented in our schools. Even within this group, however, there are some highly intellectual and creative children who are not achieving at their full potential, often because they perceive pressure at home or in school. Some of these children worry about what others think of them, and so they avoid situations where they might make mistakes.

It is important, therefore, that we as parents, grandparents and professionals realize the full value of talking to, playing with, and including our children in activities and decision making as often as possible. It is equally important that families and schools provide settings wherein creativity is encouraged, where trial and error is accepted, and where creative play is a natural part of the learning environment. If these criteria are met, the likelihood of more children demonstrating high levels of intelligence and creativity will be greatly enhanced.

The family you come from isn't as important as the family you're going to have.

—*Ring Lardner*

When talking to my own two sons I often hear his voice emerge. "If something's worth doing, it's worth doing right," Dad tells them through me. Or, "Come on, push like you mean it," when putting on their shoes. Following his lead, I don't deny myself the last piece of candy for my children's sake, with bills for self-sacrifice coming due later. And I hear echoes of my younger self when my twelve-year-old moans that his father sure can be *boring*.

—*Ralph Keyes*

Parents are people who spend the first part of a child's life getting the offspring to walk and talk and the second half trying to have the child sit down and listen.

—*Anonymous*

Little boy to playmate as a pretty girl passes by: "Boy! If I ever stop hating girls, she's the one I'll stop hating first!"

—*Anonymous*

Children are educated by what the grown-up is and not by his talk.

—*C. G. Jung*

Fathers and sons are much more considerate of one another than mothers and daughters.

—*Friedrich Wilhelm Nietzsche*

Many a parent scolds a child for things his or her own parents should have scolded for.

—*Eva Shaw*

Children alone have the temerity to trifle with the rules that generations of unimaginative adults have laid down.

—*Sister Mary Jean Dorcy*

The persons hardest to convince they're at the retirement age are children at bedtime.

—*Shannon Fife*

My mother loved children—she would have given anything if I had been one.

—*Groucho Marx*

Parents' Pledge to Their Children
from Mothercraft

From the earliest infancy we will give you our love, so that you may grow with trust in yourself and in others.

We will recognize your worth as a person and we will help you to strengthen your sense of belonging.

We will respect your right to be yourself and at the same time help you to understand the rights of others, so that you may experience cooperative living.

We will help you to develop initiative and imagination, so that you may have the opportunity freely to create.

We will encourage your curiosity and your pride in workmanship, so that you may have the satisfaction that comes from achievement.

We will provide the conditions for wholesome play that will add to your learning, to your social experience and to your happiness.

We will illustrate by precept and example the value of integrity and the importance of moral courage.

We will encourage you always to seek the truth.

We will provide you with the opportunities possible to develop your own faith in God.

We will open the way for you to enjoy the arts and to use them for deepening your understanding of life.

We will work to rid ourselves of prejudices and discrimination, so that together we may achieve a truly democratic society.

We will work to lift the standard of living and to improve our economic practices, so that you may have the material basis for a full life.

We will provide you with rewarding educational opportunities, so that you may develop your talents and contribute to a better world.

We will protect you against exploitation and undue hazards and help you grow in health and strength.

We will work to conserve and improve family life and, as needed, to provide foster care according to your inherent rights.

We will intensify our search for new knowledge in order to guide you more effectively as you develop your potentialities.

As you grow from child to youth to adult, establishing a family life of your own and accepting larger social responsibilities, we will work with you to improve conditions for all children and you.

[Editor's Note: *This pledge to children was adopted by 6,000 delegates at the Midcentury White House Conference on Children and Youth, December 3-7, 1950.*]

Little House in the Big Woods
by Laura Ingalls Wilder

The best time of all was at night when Pa came home.

He could come in from his tramping through the snowy woods with tiny icicles hanging on the ends of his mustache. He would hang his gun over the door, throw off his fur cap and coat and mittens and call:

"Where's my little half-pint of sweet cider half drunk up?"

That was Laura, because she was so small.

Laura and Mary would run to climb on his knees and sit there while he warmed himself by the fire.

All alone in the wild Big Woods, and the snow, and the cold, the little log house was warm and snug and cosy. Pa and Ma and Mary and Laura and Baby Carrie were comfortable and happy there, especially at night.

Then the fire was shining on the hearth, the cold and the dark and the wild beasts were all shut out, and Jack the brindle bulldog and Susan the black cat lay blinking at the flames in the fireplace.

Ma sat in her rocking chair, sewing by the light of the lamp on the table. The lamp was bright and shiny. There was salt in the bottom of its glass bowl with the kerosene, to keep the kerosene from exploding, and there were bits of red flannel among the salt to make it pretty. It was pretty.

Laura loved to look at the lamp, with its glass chimney so clean and sparkling, its yellow flame burning so steadily, and its bowl of clear kerosene colored red by the bits of flannel. She loved to look at the fire in the fireplace, flickering and changing all the time, burning yellow and red and sometimes green above the logs, and hovering blue over the golden and ruby coals.

And then, Pa told stories.

When Pa told a story, Laura and Mary shivered and snuggled closer to him. They were safe and snug on his knees, with his strong arms around them.

They liked to be there, before the warm fire with Susan the cat purring on the hearth and Jack the dog stretched out beside her. When they heard a wolf howl, Jack's head lifted and the hairs rose stiff along his back. But Laura and Mary listened to that lonely sound in the dark and the cold of the Big Woods, and they were not afraid.

They were cosy and comfortable in their little house made of logs, with the snow drifted around it and the wind crying because it could not get in by the fire.

Children today love luxury too much. They have execrable manners, flaunt authority, have no respect for their elders. They no longer rise when their parents or teachers enter the room. What kind of awful creatures will they be when they grow up?

—*Socrates, c. 399 B.C.*

The best way to keep children home is to make the home atmosphere pleasant—and let the air out of their tires.

—*Dorothy Parker*

You can learn many things from children. How much patience you have, for instance.

—*Franklin P. Jones*

A mother who is a mother is never free.

—*Honoré de Balzac*

The first and finest lesson that parents can teach their children is faith and courage.

—*Smiley Blanton, M.D.*

It is not possible for one to teach others who cannot teach his own family.

—*Confucius*

If there are no books in this world, then nothing need be said, but since there are books, they must be read; if there is no wine, then nothing need be said, but since there is wine, it must be drunk; if there are no famous hills, then nothing must be said, but since there are, they must be visited; if there are no flowers and no moon, then nothing need be said, but since there are, they must be enjoyed; if there are no precious children, then nothing must be said, but since there are, they must be loved and protected.

—*Chinese Proverb*

A "no" averts seventy troubles.

—*Indian Proverb*

What an act of faith it takes to have the first grandchild!

— Teresa Bloomingdale

Who among us is mature enough for offspring before the offspring themselves arrive? The value of marriage is not that adults produce children but that children produce adults.

— Peter de Vries

Instant availability without continuous presence is probably the best role a parent can play.

— Anonymous

The family is the nucleus of civilization.

— Will and Ariel Durant

Tough Questions

by Sheila Kitzinger and Celia Kitzinger

When we talk with children about things that matter we are also dealing with our own childhood. We look back to injustices we experienced—the times when we told the truth and it wasn't believed, the times we were blamed and were not responsible, the many occasions on which we were humiliated and resolved never to inflict this upon anyone else. We remember the positive experiences, too—being free to explore in the countryside or play hopscotch and ball games in the street, for example, belonging to a close-knit extended family and celebrating family festivals with aunts, uncles and grandparents—and we may feel sad that we can offer these things to our children only as our own treasured memories. We sift through the values we learned, or those we felt were inflicted upon us, as children, reinterpreting them in terms of our adult priorities and changing world.

The speed of change—new technology, new diseases, new threats and new opportunities—must make us reflect carefully on everything we are trying to teach our children. For one thing is sure: they will not inhabit a society identical to that into which we were born, and by the time they are into their twenties or thirties it may have changed beyond recognition. They will need the flexibility, courage and the strong personal values both to see and to adapt to new challenges, and to strive with others to find solutions to environmental and human problems that may appear overwhelming.

Gifts and Treasures

by Lanie Carter

Grandchildren love the way Grandma smells. I have been using the same type of perfume for years, and one time when the children were leaving, my eldest grandchild, who loved to sit on my lap, said, "I don't want to leave because I will miss the way Grandma smells."

On hearing that innocent plea, I quickly ran into the bedroom for a piece of cloth, stuffed cotton for a head, and tied a bow around the neck to make a doll. Then I sprayed the doll with my perfume, and gave it to my granddaughter.

She is fifteen years old now, and to this day every time she comes to visit, she brings the doll to get a couple of squirts of my perfume for it. Sometimes when I talk to her on the phone, she reminds me that it has been too long since our last visit because her doll has lost all of its smell.

The reminder of her love and how much she misses me is a subtle but powerful one.

A child becomes an adult when he or she walks around a puddle of water instead of through it.

—*Anonymous*

A three-year-old "big" sister constantly supervised Mom as the mother changed the newborn. After one rushed session, completed without the typical sprinkling of corn starch, the child corrected Mom: "Wait, you forgot to salt him!"

—*Anonymous*

Kids cannot choose the family in which they are raised any more than they can choose to be born male or female, black or white, rich or poor. But how children experience each of these realities is determined by the way we adults evaluate our often unexamined assumptions about different social attributes or family compositions. And just as children suffer from sexism and racism, they also hurt when their families are discredited—either directly or by inference or innuendo. Kids internalize societal criticism. They feel personally stigmatized. They blame themselves for not living "Dick and Jane" lives. They blame their parents for not being Mary Poppins or Doctor Doolittle.

—*Letty Cottin Pogrebin*

If we are ever to reach the lives of those millions of street children in our world today, we must first acquire the understanding that comes from touching one life at a time.

—Peter Taçon

Parents of young children should realize that few people, and maybe none, will find their children as enchanting as they do.

—Barbara Walters

To be closer to God, be closer to children.

—Eva Shaw

Children require guidance and sympathy far more than instruction.

—Anne Sullivan

A small child's definition of conscience: Something that makes you tell your mother before somebody else does.

—Eva Shaw

The Child is the Father of Man.

— *William Wordsworth*

The little world of childhood with its familiar surroundings is a model of the greater world. The more intensively the family has stamped its character upon the child, the more it will tend to feel and see its earlier miniature world again in the bigger world of adult life. Naturally this is not a conscious, intellectual process.

—*C. G. Jung*

What do girls do who haven't any mothers to help them through their troubles?

—*Louisa May Alcott*

What feels so nice as a child's hand in yours? So small, so soft and warm, like a kitten huddling in the shelter of your clasp.

—*Marjorie Holmes*

Farmer Smith had one of the finest apple orchards in the state, and come fall, regular as clockwork, the kids from the neighborhood would sneak in to steal apples. Regularly, too, the crusty old farmer would come charging angrily out of his house, waving a broom or even (rumor had it) a toilet plunger. He'd yell and threaten the fleeing youths with everything he could think of, including: "I'm going to call your parents!"

A new neighbor watched patiently for most of the fall and then approached the farmer. "I just don't understand you, Fred. You love kids and your grandkids never seem to get enough of being with you—and besides, you're generous and you've got ten times as many apples ripening in that orchard as you can possibly use. Why don't you just invite the school kids over to pick some?"

"Heck," laughed the farmer, pretending not to see a small group of children sneaking into the southern portion of the orchard. "I want them to have the apples, see, but I was a kid once and I know, if I didn't holler and chase them away, they'd never come back."

—Anonymous

It never occurs to a boy that someday he will be as dumb as his father.

—Mark Twain

The very world rests on the breath of children in the schoolhouse.

— The Talmud

Every Child

by *Edna Casler Joll*

Every child should know a hill,
And the clean joy of running down its long slope
With the wind in his hair.
He should know a tree —
The comfort of its cool lap of shade,
And the supple strength of its arms
Balancing him between earth and sky
So he is the creature of both.
He should know bits of singing water —
The strange mysteries of its depths,
And the long sweet grasses that border it.
Every child should know some scrap
Of uninterrupted sky, to shout against;
And have one star, dependable and bright
For wishing on.

Making the decision to have a child—it's momentous. It is to decide forever to have your heart go walking around outside your body.

—*Elizabeth Stone*

Home is the definition of God.

—*Emily Dickinson*

Future Shock Has Got Me Shooked
by *Teresa Bloomingdale*

If I had it to do over, would I raise them differently? Yes, because every mother makes mistakes and it would be foolish not to rectify them.

If I had it to do over, I'd yell less and touch more. Yelling accomplishes nothing but a sore throat (Mother's), for kids have audiometers that automatically turn off the moment a mother's voice reaches a certain decibel level. The louder she yells the less they hear.

Touching is so important, whether it be a gentle swat on the padded bottom of a stubborn two-year-old, a spontaneous hug for an exuberant ten-year-old, or the mere touch of hand to the cheek of a troubled teenager. Yes, I think I would touch my children more, though I might vary the procedures occasionally, to hug the babies and swat the teenagers.

If I had it to do over, I would spend more time reading aloud to my children, so they would become familiar with the classics, and so they would remember their mother's voice saying something other than: "It's time to get up!"

If I had it to do over, I would do it more slowly; I would take life at a more leisurely pace. While I have been rushing around the house, cleaning and cooking and searching and scolding, my kids have been growing up. Why didn't I take time out to watch?

If I had it to do over, I would never tell my children to "stay out of the living room," or "stay off the lawn," or "don't use the good dishes," or "don't touch my best towels," for this is their home, and no guests will ever be more important than my children.

If I had it to do over, I would spend more time with my children, listening to them, loving them . . . if I had it to do over.

If I had it to do over? What am I saying? With ten children, I am doing it over, and over, and over . . .

Prayer for the Children

by Francis Cardinal Spellman

Somewhere, the place it matters not—somewhere
I saw a child hungry with thin of face,
Eyes in whose pool life's joy no longer stirred
Lips that were dead to laughter's eager kiss,
Yet parted fiercely to a crust of bread.
And since that time I walk in ceaseless dread,
Fear that the child I saw, and all the hosts
Of children of a world at play with death
May die, or living, live in bitterness . . .
O God, today, above the cries of war,
Hear then thy children's prayer, and grant to us
Thy peace—God's peace
And bread for starving children!

Bibliography

Alcott, Louisa M. "Little Women Plan Christmas." From *Little Women*, included in *Story and Verse for Children*. Edited by Miriam Blanton Humber. New York: MacMillan, 1965.

Armstrong, Mildred Bowers. "Strange." In *One Thousand Beautiful Things*. Chicago: People's Book Club, 1947.

Atkins, Edith Lesser, ed. *Complete Book of Mothercraft*. New York: Greystone Press, 1952.

Beck, Alan. "What Is a Girl," *et al.* In Simpson's *Contemporary Quotations*. Boston: Houghton Mifflin Co., 1988.

Bettelheim, Bruno. *A Good Enough Parent*. New York: Alfred A. Knopf, 1987.

"A Bit of Newspaper Verse." In *Heart Throbs*. Boston: Chappler Publishing, 1905. From the National Magazine Contest, August 31, 1906.

Blessing, Kenneth R., Ph.D. "No Recipe for Creativity." In *Child's Mind, Child's Body*. New York: Council on Family Health, 1979.

Bloomingdale, Teresa. "Future Shock Has Got Me Shocked." In *I Should Have Seen It Coming When the Rabbit Died*. New York: Doubleday, 1979.

217

Carter, Lanie. "Gifts and Treasures." In *Congratulations!* New York: Pocket Books, 1990.

Children's Television Network. *Raising Kids in a Changing World.* New York: Prentice Hall, 1991.

Cosby, William H. Jr. *Childhood.* New York: Putnam, 1991.

Day, Clarence. *The Best of Life with Father.* New York: Borzoi Books, 1948.

Feiden, Karyn. *Parents' Guide to Raising Responsible Kids.* New York: Prentice Hall, 1991.

Fish, Betty, M.S.W., and Raymond Fish, Ph.D., M.D. *Letting Go.* White Hall, Va.: Betterway Publications, 1988.

"A Good Friend." In *Heart Throbs.* Boston: Chappler Publishing, 1905. From the National Magazine Contest, August 31, 1906.

Guest, Edgar A. *Just Folks.* New York: Reilly & Britton, 1917.

Hasley, Lucile. "A Little Peach in the Orchard Grew," by S. J. Sheed. In *The New Guest Room Book.* Kansas City, Mo.: Sheed & Ward, 1957.

Hernandez, Marcos Behean. "Five Ways." In *Communicating with Our Sons and Daughters.* Rockville, Md.: National Institute on Drug Abuse, U.S. Department of Health and Human Services, 1980.

"His Father Is Satisfied." In *Heart Throbs.* Boston: Chappler Publishing, 1905. From *Chicago Advance* (newspaper), c. 1885.

Jackson, Shirley. "How to Perfect Maternal Feelings of Guilt." In *Special Delivery.* New York: Little, Brown/McCall Corporation, 1959.

Joll, Edna Casler. "Every Child." In *One Thousand Beautiful Things.* Chicago: People's Book Club, 1947.

Keller, Helen. "The World Through Three Senses." *Ladies' Home Journal,* March 1951.

Kitzinger, Sheila, and Celia Kitzinger. *Tough Questions: Talking Straight with Your Kids About the Real World.* Boston: The Harvard Common Press, 1991.

Knox, Msgr. Ronald. "Our Lady Teaches Her Son," a BBC talk on children and religion. In *The Gospel in Slow Motion,* 1953.

Langdon, Grace, Ph.D. "The Priceless Privilege of Parenthood." In *Complete Book of Mothercraft.* Edited by Edith Lesser Atkin, M.S. New York: Greystone Press, 1952.

Linkletter, Arthur G. "Kids Still Say the Darndest Things." In *The Secret Worlds of Kids.* New York: Bernard Geis Associates, 1959.

———. "Brave New Electronic World." In *Kids Sure Rite Funny!* New York: Bernard Geis Associates, 1962.

"A Lonesome Boy." *The New York Times,* 2 September 1900.

Lubbock, John. "What Makes a Home?" In *One Thousand Beautiful Things.* Chicago: People's Book Club, 1947.

Prudden, Bonnie. "The Starting Line." In *Fitness from Six to Twelve.* New York: Dial Press, 1972.

Rhodes, Cecil. "A Child's Legacy." In *One Thousand Beautiful Things.* Chicago: People's Book Club, 1947.

Rich, Dorothy. "Inspiration and Perspiration." In *Megaskills.* Boston: Houghton Mifflin, 1988.

Roeske, Nancy C. A., M.D. "Problems of Sterotyped Sex Roles." In *Child's Mind, Child's Body.* New York: Council on Family Health, 1979.

Rogers, Fred, and Barry Head. *Mister Rogers Talks with Parents.* New York: Family Communications, 1983.

Ross, Alice. "A Letter to My Chosen Child." *Family Newspaper,* January 1995.

Salk, Lee. *The Complete Dr. Salk.* New York: New American Library, 1983.

Saraswati, Shantanand. "The Letters of Love." In *Pure Wisdom.* Costa Mesa, Calif.: Allwon, 1992.

Schulman, Michael. *The Passionate Mind.* New York: Free Press, 1991.

Schulman, Michael, and Eva Mekler. *Bringing Up a Moral Child.* Reading, Mass.: Addison-Wesley Publishing, 1985.

Siegler, Ava L. *What Should I Tell the Kids?* New York: Dutton, 1993.

"The Timeless House of Children's Games." *Sports Illustrated,* 26 December 1960.

Vitello, Paul, and Carol Polsky. "Raising Good Kids in a World That's Not." *Woman's Day,* 4 April 1995: 60-63.

Whitham, Cynthia. *Win the Whining War & Other Skirmishes.* Los Angeles: Perspective Publishing, 1991.

Wilder, Laura Ingalls. "Little House in the Big Woods." In *Little House in the Big Woods.* New York: Harper and Row, 1932.

Wolf, Anna W. M. "Growing Up." In *A Reader for Parents.* New York: W. W. Norton, 1963.

Wyse, Lois. "I Remember Grandma." In *Grandchildren Are So Much Fun I Should Have Had Them First.* New York: Crown Publishing, 1992.

Index of Authors

Index of Titles

Chicken Soup for the whole family

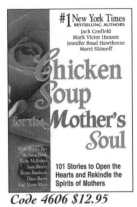

Code 4606 $12.95

Code 4630 $12.95

The Braids Girl

When Izzy helps Grandpa Mike with his volunteer work at the Family Togetherness Home, the girl in the corner with the two long braids makes a lasting impression on her. . .

Code 5548, hardcover, $14.95

A Dog of My Own

Ben's dearest wish comes true when his mom finally consents to his long-standing plea for a puppy. But, on the way to pick up a picture perfect puppy, Ben and his friend Kelly stumble upon a discovery that could change everything!

Code 5556, hardcover, $14.95